CW01574861

The Jigsa
Mysteries

SOUTH AFRICA

Elaine Wallace

To Dylan and Ben,

Happy reading!

Elaine

Copyright © Elaine Wallace 2024

The moral right of Elaine Wallace to be identified as the author of this work has been asserted in accordance with the Copyright, Designs and Patents Act 1988.

All rights reserved. No part of this book may be reproduced or used in any manner whatsoever, including information storage and retrieval systems, or transmitted in any form or by any means, electronic, mechanical, photocopying, recording or otherwise, without the express written permission of the copyright owner, except in the case of brief quotations embodied in critical reviews and certain other non-commercial use permitted by copyright law. For permission requests, contact the author at the address below.

This is a work of fiction and any places, businesses, events and incidents in this book are used in a fictitious manner.

First edition printed and published in the United Kingdom 2024 by Orry Publishing.

A CIP catalogue record of this book is available from the British Library.

ISBN: 978-1-7384392-0-1 (Paperback)

ISBN: 978-1-7384392-1-8 (eBook)

Illustrated by Emily Wallace

Typesetting and Design by Debra Murphy

For further information about this book, please contact the author at: e-wallace.co.uk

This book is dedicated to my wonderful husband, Craig, and beautiful children, Emily, Christopher and Rebecca who shared my incredible adventures in South Africa and made it a magical experience.

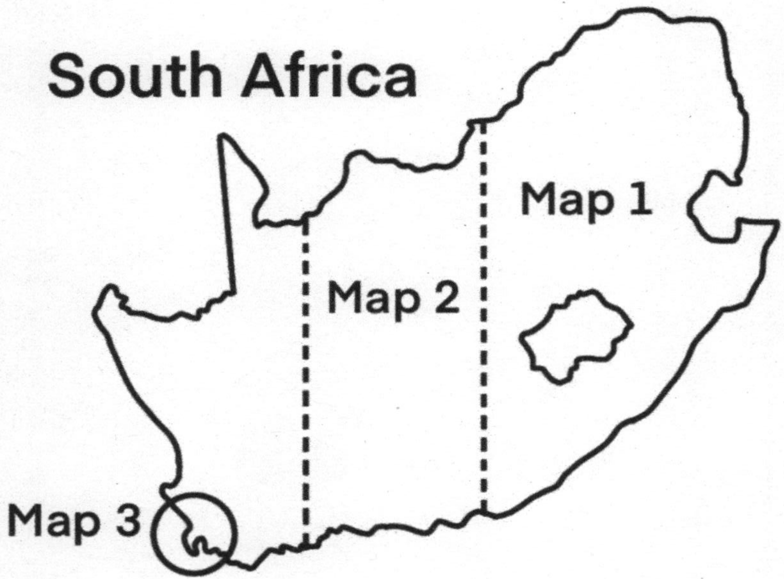
South Africa
Map 1
Map 2
Map 3

Prologue

As the evening settled over the small, sleepy village of Eaglesville, a slight disturbance broke the silence. The wind was making the leaves rustle, the flag on its pole was moving slightly and the water in the stream was babbling softly. Tap! Then it sounded again. Tap, tap. It wasn't obvious where the noise was coming from, and at first glance, everything appeared to be still.

Suddenly there came an almighty, ear-deafening shriek which filled the silence. Almost immediately, a fog descended over the village. The fog was so thick that nothing was visible. Footsteps. Silence.

Then bit by bit, more footsteps. Out of the fog appeared a figure dressed entirely in black apart from its face, surrounded by a hood. On closer inspection, the figure's face was deathly white, withered and emaciated.

It spoke in a whisper, "Who has dared to awaken me?"

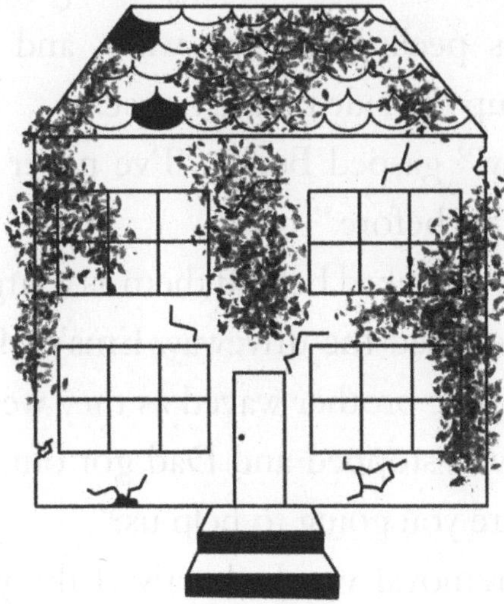

Chapter 1

"I'm going to get there first!" shouted Becks to the other two who were racing behind her.

"We're catching you up!" screamed Ems.

Rich, trying his best, had slowed down to a slight jog. As they approached the driveway to the house, they all stopped.

"I can't believe you're going to live here, Ems," said Rich.

"I know," replied Ems. "I don't know what possessed them to buy such a ramshackle place."

The house itself was hidden behind a mass of trees and bushes. The driveway was barely passable with all the weeds growing there. The paint was peeling off the walls, and ivy was growing up the side of the house.

"Wow!" gasped Becks. "I've never been as close as this before."

A horn honked behind them as a large white van approached the driveway. Ems's Mum and Dad and little brother waved as they went by.

The van stopped and Dad got out. "Right, you lot, are you going to help us?"

The removal van had arrived the previous day with all the large items which had already been unloaded.

Dad unlocked the door and let Ems and her friends in to explore.

A large staircase with an ornate banister faced them as they entered the house. To the left was a sitting room with an enormous, old fireplace. Beyond that was an ancient kitchen which looked like it was from the Victorian era. To the right was another sitting room, and behind that, a bathroom and a large cupboard.

Giggling as they went upstairs, the three children looked out of the window at the top in amazement. The immaculate garden below them wouldn't have been out of place in one of those glossy country magazines.

The back garden was huge and perfect. Cobbled paths ran through a maze of small, manicured areas. Roses climbed high up the brick wall, different coloured shrubs and bushes were dotted around and in the middle was a large statue. From where they were looking, they couldn't quite make out what it depicted.

"Let's quickly look around here and head out to explore the garden!" exclaimed Rich.

"It looks amazing. Why do you think the previous owner looked after the garden and let the rest of the house get into such a mess?" asked Becks.

"I'm not sure," replied Ems. "We'll need to ask my mum and dad later."

Upstairs there were three large bedrooms and a smaller study with a tiny staircase going off it.

"Where does that go?" wondered Becks when she found the small door at the top was locked.

"I'll ask about that too. I wonder what's inside. I bet there's a ghost living there. Wooooo!" answered Ems laughing.

"Let's hope not," said Becks, looking worried.

The three of them ran downstairs eagerly, wanting to explore the garden. They found an old, rusty key in the back door. Turning the key, they opened it slowly. Once through the creaking door they found themselves in a tranquil paradise that had been hidden for so long behind the derelict house. Running straight towards the statue in the middle, they realised it was of a young man clutching a box. He appeared to be bent over staring at it. His handsome face had a look of longing about it. Although slightly crumbled in parts and weather-beaten, the statue was still pretty much intact.

"I wonder who he was and what was inside the box?" pondered Rich. Rich loved a puzzle - games, jigsaws, crosswords - anything that got him thinking and analysing. He also loved gaming and playing with his friends online. Ask Rich anything about geography, and he'd know the answer. Rich was only eleven years old, but he was taller than most of his friends his age. He was a friendly lad who loved pink, with a seemingly endless supply of pink tops - bright pink, salmon pink, baby pink, cerise pink - as long as it was pink, he would wear it!

With eyes opened wide in amazement, the children explored the rest of the garden. Every so often, they passed small carved stones with what appeared to be lettering and markings which looked a bit like countries.

"I wonder what these are for. There are loads of them!" exclaimed Ems. "They look like they might all fit together."

Rich grabbed the one in front of him and tried to move it, but it was no use. It didn't look particularly heavy, but there was no budging it.

Examining it closely, Rich said, "I think the rocks look like jigsaw pieces, even though they have been battered from the weather."

"We'll have a better look another day," said Ems. "I'd better go and help with the unpacking now. Pop round tomorrow after lunch and we can explore some more. See you later."

Rich and Becks both said goodbye to Ems and her family and left for the evening.

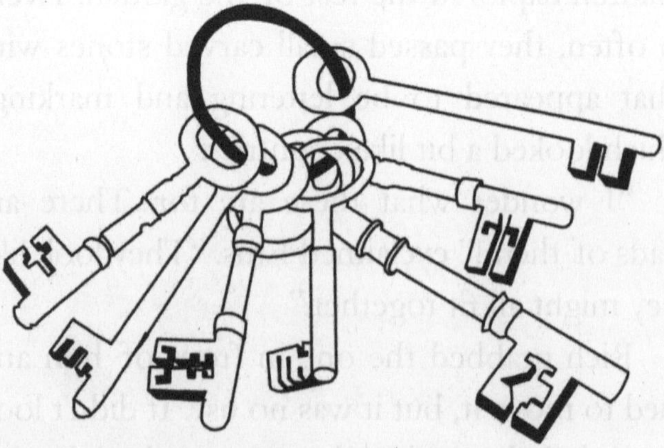

Chapter 2

Ems woke with a start in the middle of the night, wondering what had awakened her. She listened for a moment, but there was nothing other than silence. Ems got out of bed anyway and padded downstairs to the bathroom. On her way down, she passed the window on the landing, which overlooked the garden. It was an almost full moon. The statue looked somehow different in the moonlight. Ems stared at it for a moment, not quite sure what was catching her eye - but then she realised. The statue appeared to be taller than before and not quite so bent.

Shrugging her shoulders, she continued on her way to the bathroom. On the way back to her bedroom she looked out of the window again. The statue seemed to be back to normal.

I'm sure it's just my eyes playing tricks on me or the moon's shadows, she thought. Back she went to her warm, comfy bed.

The following day Ems got to work unpacking all her belongings into the huge wardrobe and cupboards in her room. She lined up all her graphic oversized t-shirts and hoodies that she loved to wear, along with trainers and baggy joggers, on her wardrobe rails. Her room for the moment was immaculate but given a few days would resemble a scene out of a disaster movie. Ems looked around her, pleased with herself and started to hang her animal posters on the walls. She was a great animal lover, and her collection of both printed posters and her own drawings was something she was very proud of.

Ems went down for some lunch with her parents and her little brother. Jackson was five years old and absolutely doted on his big sister. He loved to be around Ems, but Ems being ten years old, found this slightly irritating sometimes. She enjoyed hanging out with her friends and hated it when Jackson had to tag along.

"Dad, do you know who owned this house before and why they looked after the back garden but not the rest of it?" enquired Ems.

"It belonged to Mr Whitworth. Remember, he used to walk along to the shops pulling a wee black trolley? He was a nice man who always said hello but never stopped for a conversation. We didn't realise what the garden was like until we saw the house. Nobody had passed the front entrance for years, and you can't see the back garden at all as it's so enclosed. It's such a shame as the garden is so beautiful. It should have been there for people to admire," explained Dad.

"The statue of the boy is interesting. I'm not sure what he's holding. It looks like a box, and there are small rocks dotted about the garden too," carried on Ems. "Do you know where the key is for the attic door? It's locked!"

"It might be in this huge bundle," said Dad pointing to a rusty, old pile of keys.

"I'll try them if you want and see if I can find the correct one," said Ems enthusiastically.

"Great," replied Dad. "That will be something less to do. We're hoping to get the last of the boxes emptied today, and then we can start decorating the lounge."

"Just be careful if you manage to find the key and open the door. We don't know what's up there!" said Mum.

"We will, Mum. Don't worry!" answered Ems.

Ems waited for her friends to arrive, taking the heavy bundle of keys with her. They were all different types: large, small, gold, silver and all rusted.

"What have you got there?" shouted Becks as she rode up the driveway on her much-loved purple bike.

Rich followed behind her on his black bike with a tiny bit of pink writing just visible.

"Dad found a huge bundle of keys. The only problem is finding which one actually opens the attic door!" replied Ems.

Rich and Becks propped their bikes against the wall, and the three of them went into the house and up the stairs to the attic door.

Ems went through the keys one at a time. Try after try, key after key, but none of them fitted.

"We're down to the last two. Please, let one of these be the key!" Ems said, looking in despair.

The last key fitted into the lock, and with a sigh of relief, Ems easily turned it and began to open the attic door.

Chapter 3

The door was very old and heavy, and as Ems pushed her shoulder against it, the door creaked open, and the three children entered the room. They stood open-mouthed at the scene that was in front of them.

From floor to ceiling were piles of belongings: huge cardboard boxes stacked up tall, rails of clothes - dresses, jumpers, coats - enormous chests, battered suitcases and loads of cobwebs dangling from the ceiling.

"Look at this stuff!" exclaimed Becks. "Your parents are going to be ages sorting out all this."

"I know," Ems replied.

Rich ventured forward. There was a path without any clutter going through the centre of the attic. They walked cautiously through it, looking about with interest at all that was there. Light flooded in from the attic windows, projecting shadows across the ceiling.

"Watch out for the spiders' webs," Becks said with a shudder. "I don't want any to land on my head!"

Becks was the sporty one of the three. Whatever the sport, Becks loved to play. Leggings, t-shirts and trainers were her everyday fashion. She had always loved playing football and enjoyed nothing more than going to see the local football team with her dad when she saw him every other weekend.

Becks lived with her mum most of the time in a flat in the village. Her dad lived just on the outskirts in a small, old house that he was in the process of doing up.

Rich started to look through one of the open boxes. Lots of old-fashioned toys were in it - dolls, teddy bears and wooden blocks - which had obviously been well used.

"Look at these!" he said to the others. "They are so old that they should be in a museum like that one in Edinburgh."

"They smell a bit too," said Ems, holding her nose as she started to look through one of the rails of clothes.

The three of them tried on some of the old jackets, parading around in them and laughing at each other as they each took a turn walking down the 'catwalk'.

Once they had put the clothes back on the rail, Becks emptied out one of the chests which was full of games and puzzles.

"Look at these Rich, you will love what's inside this chest," said Becks.

Rich went over and looked through the bundle from the box. Amongst others were chess, draughts, dominoes, backgammon and some jigsaw puzzles.

"These are great. Do you want to play dominoes?" Rich asked the others.

They managed to clear a space and started to play the game. Whilst playing, Rich kept on looking over at one of the jigsaw puzzles.

"What do you keep looking at?" asked Ems.

"That jigsaw just looks really familiar. I feel like I've seen it before somewhere," Rich replied.

Becks leaned over and picked the puzzle up. They all looked at the box, brows furrowing as they stared at it intently.

Rich suddenly exclaimed, "I know where I've seen it. In the garden! The rocks with the markings on them that looked like pieces of a map. This is it!"

The jigsaw puzzle had five hundred pieces and depicted a map of the world. The box was quite battered but the picture on the lid was barely marked. Ems opened the box and inside were what appeared to be all the pieces. Some were strange shapes, not like the typical jigsaw shape.

Rich picked up a couple of the pieces.

"Let's go outside and look at the rocks and see if they really are the same," he said.

Becks lifted the box, and they all ran downstairs into the garden. They stopped by the first stone just in front of the roses. Crouching down, they examined it more closely.

"Look, the markings are the same as the ones on the jigsaw pieces. The outline of the countries is in black and then the places are written in gold. Some of the lettering has been worn away by the weather but you can still just about make out a name," said Rich.

"Will we start the jigsaw right now?" said Becks.

"Yes, let's go back to the attic and see if we can complete it," replied Ems.

They soon had all the edges completed and had finished most of the continents. An hour later, after brief messages to Rich and Becks's parents to say they would be home after dinner, they were ready to put the final pieces into the puzzle.

"Since it's your house, Ems, you can put the final piece in," said Becks. She and Rich quickly put their pieces in, which left just Ems's last piece.

"Here it goes," Ems said happily, putting the last piece in.

The piece was part of South Africa and had gold writing on it showing the country's name. Just as her fingers pushed it into the final position, there came an almighty whoosh of wind. The three children screamed as the tornado force wind raged around them. In an instant, the force of it transported them shrieking into the jigsaw.

Then the wind died down and the jigsaw remained complete on the attic floor. Ems, Rich and Becks were nowhere to be seen!

Chapter 4

The figure in black proceeded to walk, or more accurately glide, through the village, past the hotel, play park and library. Followed by the thick fog, it continued towards an old house covered with ivy, and a driveway consumed by weeds. Although the front door of the house was locked, the figure opened the door without a key and silently went upstairs into the crowded attic. It stood looking at the jigsaw left lying on the floor, complete.

"Where have they gone?" the rasping voice spoke from inside the hood. "They have no idea what they have done. They will wish they had never seen this house, never mind completed the jigsaw, by the time I find them."

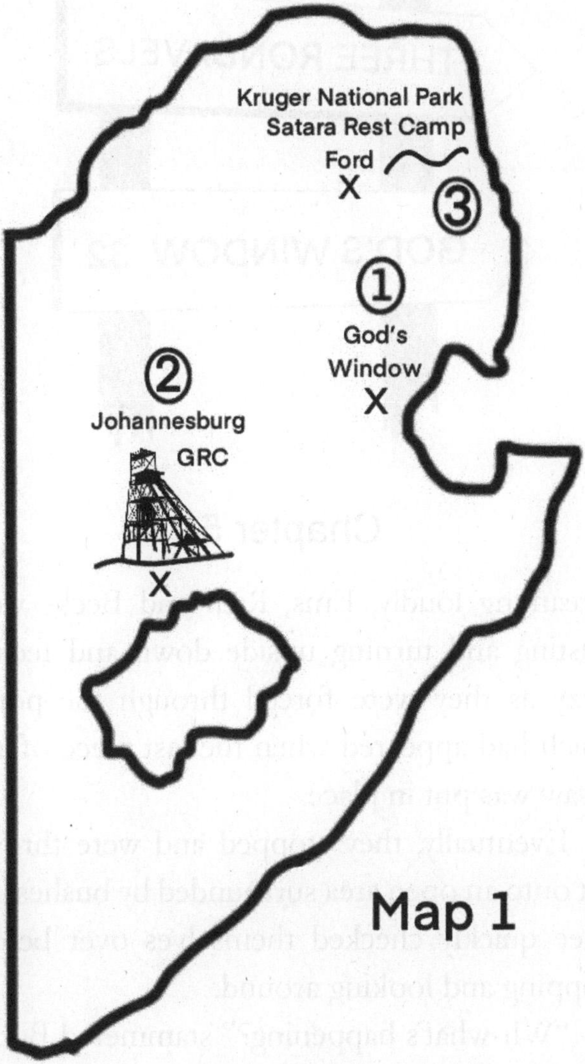
Kruger National Park
Satara Rest Camp
Ford
X
3
1
God's
Window
X
2
Johannesburg
GRC
X
Map 1

Chapter 5

Screaming loudly, Ems, Rich and Becks were twisting and turning upside down and feeling dizzy as they were forced through the portal which had appeared when the last piece of the jigsaw was put in place.

Eventually, they stopped and were thrown out onto an open area surrounded by bushes. All three quickly checked themselves over before stopping and looking around.

"Wh-what's happening?" stammered Becks.

"I'm not sure. Where are we and how did we get here?" Ems answered, sounding puzzled.

Rich stood up and started to survey the area around them. Ahead of them were three oddly shaped hills with sharp sides and domed tops with gentle slopes.

Scratching his head and rubbing his eyes in disbelief, Rich opened and then closed his mouth, trying to speak. He tried again.

"I think when we put that last piece of the puzzle in, something happened to open a portal to bring us here. I'm not one hundred per cent sure but I think we may be in South Africa."

The other two looked at him, scarcely believing what they were hearing.

"Are you sure? You don't think this is just a stupid dream and we're going to wake up any minute?" Becks said in a whimpering voice. Ems nodded in agreement.

"You know how I've been interested in that map game online. Well, it has pictures of landmarks from around the world and I'm sure that this was one from South Africa. We are in Blyde River Canyon which is one of the biggest canyons in the world," Rich replied.

Ems suddenly felt something in her pocket, put her hand in and brought out a folded piece of paper.

"Where has this come from?" she said to the others, unfolding the paper, with the other two looking over her shoulder. It was a map of South Africa.

"What do we need to do with it?" said Becks, still looking worried.

They looked at it closely. It was detailed with place names - Cape Town, Johannesburg, Kruger National Park - and had numbers dotted around the map.

"How are we going to get home?" said Becks in a scared whisper.

"I'm not sure," replied Rich. "I think we need to follow the directions on the map."

"Do you think anyone has noticed we're missing yet?" said Becks.

"I think it will be a couple of hours, because Mum and Dad think we're upstairs in the attic doing a jigsaw," answered Ems.

Rich turned the map over and saw that on the back of it there was faint writing.

"There's a message on the back," he said. Rich read the words out. "Don't tell anyone you are here. Follow the directions on the map and then you will be able to go home. If you don't complete the challenge, then a huge number of monstrous figures will be unleashed. You have already awoken the first. Join together all the pieces of the jigsaw and you will be able to go home. When you find the pieces of the puzzle they act as a portal to get you from one destination to another. If you all touch it together and say where you want to go, it will take you within a couple of miles of it. You can use this map as the first one."

"M-m-monstrous f-figures," stammered Becks. "Do you think this is real?"

"I'm not willing to take any chances," said Ems.

At that moment, in the silence, a rasping voice was heard. It just seemed to be in the air around them.

"Where are they?" it rasped menacingly.

"Who's there?" screamed Becks.

Silence. They could only hear the sound of their own breathing and the chirping of the crickets and birds.

"What do we do now? We can't even call home to let them know we're safe," said Ems.

"I think we need to do what it says on the back of the map," said the ever-sensible Rich.

"Look, we know where we are. We just need to follow these clues, use the jigsaw pieces and then we'll be home before we know it."

"Right, let's focus then," said Becks. "What do you think it means by clues?"

The three of them studied the map.

Ems replied, "It looks like we need to find the jigsaw pieces. There are ten numbers on the map, so it appears we need to find them all."

"How will we know exactly where they are?" asked Becks.

"I'm hoping when we get to the first it will be pretty obvious," said Rich. "The first one is definitely within Blyde River Canyon. I'm certain that we're at the Three Rondavels, and it looks like the first one is called God's Window."

"What's that?" said Ems.

"I have absolutely no idea," replied Rich. "We can use the map to get there."

"Wherever that voice came from I want to get as far away from it as possible. Let's leave here now," urged Becks.

They had a last look at the beautiful view in front of them and then started walking towards the road. They walked in silence, each absorbed in their own thoughts. When they got to the road, having passed nobody on the way, they were fortunate to see a sign pointing to the Three Rondavels. That same sign showed the mileage to God's Window.

"Oh, thank goodness! At least we've found the sign, but it's a long way off," Rich panted.

They walked in single file, Becks at the front, then Ems and Rich following at the back. Each of them was trying to process the happenings of the last hour. They walked for a while before stopping.

"I think we're far enough away from that awful voice to have a rest. Let's stop and see whether we can access the portal and get to God's Window," suggested Ems.

"Great idea," answered Rich. "It's tiring walking."

Stopping at the side of the road, they took out the map.

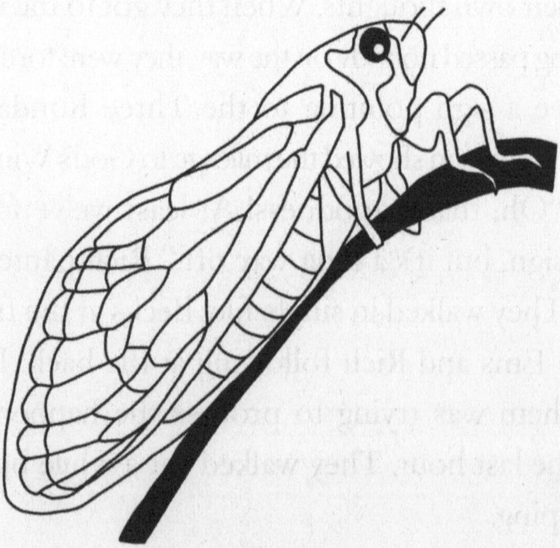

Chapter 6

They stared at the map wondering how to use it. "Let's all place our finger on it, say 'God's Window' and see what happens," said Ems, shrugging her shoulders.

Kneeling with the map on the ground, they all placed a finger on it and at the same time shouted, "God's Window."

Whoosh! The same sensation as before. Twisting and turning as they travelled through the portal. Landing with a bump, the three children dusted themselves off and had a good look at their surroundings.

The landscape in front of them was green and rocky in parts. A sign pointed to God's Window.

"Look! It's just up that path," Rich announced as he started walking.

On either side of the path was a myriad of plants, shrubs and bushes. The children had never seen such variety before, different shades of green, tiny waxy leaves, enormous leaves, small pockets of colourful flowers and huge trees.

The path was quite uneven, and the children all had to watch their step as it wound its way up beneath the canopy of trees. Birds were calling and chirping, geckos scuttled under the rocks and eagles and falcons hovered and swooped overhead beyond the tops of the trees.

Ems paused to look at one of the tiny geckos.

"Look at it, it's so cute," cooed Ems. "The spotted pattern means it can camouflage itself. I think they eat insects too instead of plants."

Just at that moment, everything around the children fell silent. Not a sound could be heard anywhere. No movement amidst the trees, no birds chirping, no insects moving.

All of a sudden they could hear a noise. It started off as a slight buzzing sound but gradually became louder and louder.

"Where's that noise coming from?" wondered Rich. "It sounds like a motorbike, but we are quite a distance from the road now."

Ems moved back down the path a few metres to see if she could spot anything.

"It's definitely louder down here," she said, looking puzzled.

At that moment, she started to waft something away, and shrieked, "Ugh, there's a massive bug flying around me! It's like a locust."

The next moment, she turned and started to run up the path towards Rich and Becks who were still standing together.

"There's lots of them coming!" she screamed. "Run!"

Instantly, in the place where Ems had been standing, there came a sea of insects. The noise was so loud, it was ear piercing. Hundreds of them were flying towards the three children. Ems, Becks and Rich took to their heels and ran blindly through the forest.

"Stay on the path!" cried Becks. "If we come off it, we might not find our way back."

"Look around for somewhere to shelter," puffed Rich.

The insects were now starting to encircle them. With their arms flailing, all three children tried to swat the insects away. The sound was unbearable, they couldn't even hear each other shout. Still running, they looked around wildly for some kind of shelter. A large rock appeared in the distance. Becks waved her hands and pointed to it as best she could.

By now, several insects had landed on their clothes, and the children were trying in vain to sweep them off. As they did, more came to rest. After what seemed like an eternity, they eventually came to the rock and quickly got behind it. Crouching down, the children covered their ears as the swarm of insects passed noisily around them. Hundreds of thousands of them flew by, the noise becoming more intense as the centre of the swarm passed overhead. The children looked in wonder as these creatures passed, not having seen anything like this before. Eventually, the noise lessened, and the insects started to fade away until just a few remained.

Ems, Becks and Rich stood up, looking quite alarmed by what they had encountered, and swept the rest of the insects off their clothes.

"What on earth were those?" cried Becks, shivering. "I thought my ears were going to explode with the noise and when they landed on me, aagh!"

"They were cicadas. The noise they make is the internal tymbal muscle contracting which then produces the sound," described Ems. "I've never even seen one before, never mind heard one."

"Well, I for one, definitely do not want to see or hear those things again," replied Becks, still shaken.

One of the cicadas had landed on the tree beside them, and Ems, after looking around and seeing that there were no more, went over to have a good look at it. Cicadas have prominent eyes which are set wide apart, membranous front wings and short antennae.

"I can't believe that those insects can make such a loud noise. I can still hear it reverberating in my head," said Becks, speaking louder than usual.

"Thank goodness they only drink the sap from tree branches, roots and twigs," spoke Ems knowingly.

"Now they're gone, let's see if we can find this jigsaw piece," said Rich, starting to walk up the stony path.

The other two proceeded to walk behind him, continuing to keep a look out for the swarm of cicadas.

Eventually, a sign pointed them to the final few metres up to God's Window. Standing on a cliff seven hundred feet high, looking over the lush, vast landscape beneath them, they were awestruck by the view. A panorama of hills, forests and rock formations as far as the eye could see lay in front of them.

"What a view!" exclaimed Ems, taking it all in. "It just goes on and on."

After a few minutes, Ems started to have a look around.

"What do you think we're looking for?" she asked.

"I have no idea, but I'm wondering if the jigsaw pieces might be rocks like the ones in the garden. Let's split up and take an area each," answered Becks.

They each took an area that was a few metres wide and got down on their hands and knees to have a good look. There were lots of rocks so each one was scrutinised carefully.

Finally, Becks shouted the other two over.

"Look at this one, it has markings on it." She tried to pull it out of the ground but there was no moving it.

"Let me have a go," said Rich. He pulled at the rock and after some time it started to move. He rocked it back and forth until it became loose.

On the rock were some markings that could be a map.

"It's like the rocks in the garden back at home," Ems said excitedly. "They all have markings like this one."

"Do you think we just keep the rocks together until we find them all and we can complete the jigsaw?" asked Becks.

Rich and Ems both agreed with Becks.

"Should we use the portal again to try and get to the next jigsaw piece? I think the map said number two was in Johannesburg," suggested Rich.

"It's such a busy city, isn't it?" asked Becks. "I hope we don't get lost there."

Chapter 7

The three children put their fingers on the jigsaw piece as before, said the name, and in no time at all they were hurtling towards Johannesburg, spinning and turning, and landing with a thud. Arriving on the side of a paved area, they quickly took in their surroundings. All around them were people - couples, families, school groups - all laughing and chatting away happily.

They soon saw why there was all this merriment. They were in a theme park filled with exciting rides, stalls and food outlets. The smell coming from the food outlets was amazing -

sickly sweet aroma of waffles and doughnuts, salty chips and melted cheese on top of burgers smothered in ketchup. Rich, Becks and Ems were salivating at the smells around them.

"I'm starving!" announced Rich, looking around him, his eyes wide open at the array of food.

"Me too!" agreed Ems. "Let's get something to eat."

Becks made her way over to one of the tables outside a fast-food restaurant and sat down. The others followed, by this time realising that they had no way of paying for anything. None of them had any money in their pockets they could use.

"What are you doing?" whispered Ems. "We have no money!"

"Watch!" answered Becks as a school party sat down on the seats around them. A couple of children came over to sit at their table.

"After being on all those rides, I need something to eat, I'm so-o-o hungry," a girl with dark hair and matching shorts and t-shirt exclaimed. "Have you been on many rides yet?"

She didn't appear to be asking anyone in particular, so Becks answered.

"Not many," she said, telling a wee white lie. "We're going to get something to eat and then go on some."

They were soon served a burger and chips along with the rest of the children. Ems, Rich and Becks ate the sumptuous lunch while talking away to the children next to them. They discovered that they were the same age and that they were on a school trip there.

Rich suddenly had an idea. He got the map out of his pocket and showed them the part with Johannesburg on it.

"Can you help us find this bit on the map?" he asked.

"It's a bit faded," replied the girl who was called Palesa. "It looks like it's in the theme park itself. Look, there's the initials GRC - Gold Reef City."

"There's a small picture next to it. Look over there," said a boy called Bandile, pointing at a large bit of machinery a few metres away. "It's exactly like the picture."

Right enough, in front of them was an old piece of mining equipment used in the days when there was a gold mine there.

"You can do a tour of the mine and go down in the lift underneath the ground. You can also see the old-fashioned houses from the mining days too," said Palesa. "We're just going to go down there. Why don't you join us?"

"That would be great. We're really interested in finding out more about the mine and the gold rush," answered Rich, excitedly looking at both Ems and Becks, who were nodding enthusiastically in agreement.

At that moment, a teacher raised his hand, and the rest of the class were silent quickly. He gave the group some instructions and they all started to get into lines.

"Come and join us. There are a few kids not here today so you can come and take their places," said Bandile.

Ems, Rich and Becks quickly got into a line with Bandile and Palesa and started making their way to the old-fashioned houses.

They had a look round the houses, commenting on the differences between the houses of the mine officials in the late 1800's and houses in the present day.

"I don't think I would have liked to have lived then," Becks said. "What would they have done with no television or internet?"

"They would have worked long hours and would have played games, read, sewn, or done the cooking or cleaning. Life would have been hard back then," replied Palesa knowledgeably.

It was soon time for their turn to go down into the mine. Ems, Rich and Becks went into the lift (after putting their safety helmets on) along with their new friends and several other children. The lift doors were pulled over and they started the descent into the mine. It was noisy with the old machinery clicking and clanking as the lift slowly went down. Down and down they went, until they were seventy-five metres below the surface. The lift came to an abrupt stop and as they disembarked, they realised that it was much colder.

"It's cold down here," said Ems, shivering as she wrapped her arms around herself.

An elderly man met them all and introduced himself as Benjamin, the tour guide. He started explaining about the workings of the old mine and they began to move through it. They passed the miners' identity box where they counted the people that went down the mine, the first aid station and several cabinets with explosives in them.

Looking down one of the mine shafts, they could see that they went down for several more metres. Benjamin told them that they couldn't go any further as the levels further down were flooded and were now inaccessible. There were several mine carriages, filled to the brim with large rocks.

Rich looked at Ems and Becks in despair.

"How are we going to find the one that we need down here when there are literally hundreds of them!" he exclaimed.

"I have no idea where we would even start," Becks said, crestfallen.

By this time the group were starting to make their way back to the lift. Ems, Becks and Rich quickly hid behind one of the mine carriages. After a couple of minutes, they were left in silence as the lift ascended through the mine shafts.

"Let's have a quick look around before the next group comes down," said Rich hurriedly.

"Let's each take a carriage and start to look through it. Hopefully we'll be lucky."

They all took a separate carriage and started to go through it rock by rock. Piece after piece was placed next to the carriage after a quick inspection to rule out if it was the next jigsaw piece. It was heavy work, lifting and laying the rocks. After about twenty minutes they had finished emptying the carriages and had the painstaking job of putting them back again. They were so busy that they failed to notice that the lift had come back down.

"You lot! What are you doing down here on your own?" shouted Benjamin.

The three children looked up, alarmed at being caught. Quickly they ran down the steps in one of the open mine shafts. As they got further down, the visibility got worse. It became darker and colder. They got to the next level which was a replica of the one above that they had just left.

Standing quietly, all they could hear was their own loud breathing, and in the level above some shouts getting louder as people started to look for them.

"What are we going to do?" whispered Becks, looking nervous. "We can't get caught!"

Just before Ems could reply, there came an almighty noise from the level below them. Looking down the mine shaft behind them they could see water starting to come up the shaft. Another explosion on their right found them being hurled against the wall with such force that they were all momentarily stunned. Rubbing their heads and checking to see if each other were okay, they then peered down the corridor to see where the noise had come from.

At that moment, the ceiling just beyond them, where the explosion had been, started to collapse. Mud, rocks and stones fell in front of them, and huge dust clouds were formed. By now they couldn't see anything, and they quickly started to run in the opposite direction, the mine ceiling continuing to fall behind them as they ran. Before long they were engulfed in stones and mud. Falling, they collapsed as the overwhelming weight of the tumbling rocks sent them sprawling to the floor.

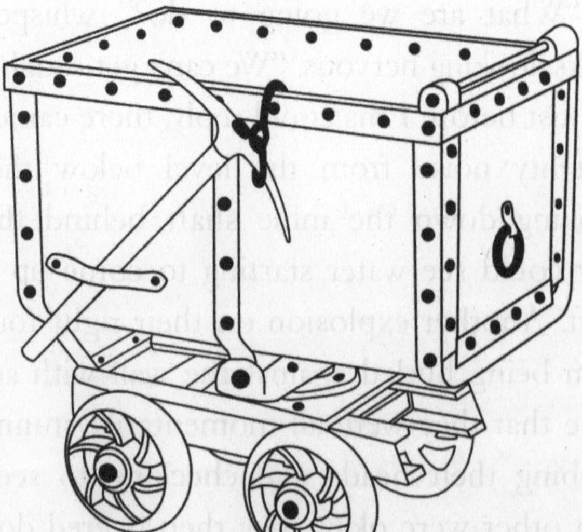

Chapter 8

Silence. Other than the sound of an occasional drip, there was only silence. The scene was one of devastation. Mud upon mud. Stone upon stone. Rock upon rock.

Suddenly, there came the noise of the shifting of some stones. Then the sound of rocks being moved one by one.

"Becks, Rich! Are you OK?" a voice said.

No answer. Then it came again.

"Becks, Rich! Are you OK?"

Finally, from a place a few metres away was a groaning noise.

"I'm coming!" shouted Ems as she moved more rocks and stones. She stood up and started to pick her way over to where the noise had come from. It was almost completely dark, apart from a faint light that came down the shaft from the upper level.

"I can't see you. Shout again!" yelled Ems.

The groaning sound came again quite close to where she was standing. Ems started digging around in the stones and rocks. As she did so, the noise got louder and louder. Finally, she could see a shoe, and moved all the rubble off the leg and the rest of the body to reveal Becks underneath.

"Are you OK?" she asked.

"I think so," answered Becks as she checked herself over. "Just a bit sore and I have some cuts, but I don't think anything's broken. Where's Rich?"

"I don't know. I haven't heard any other noises down here," replied Ems.

"Oh! I hope he's okay," said Becks as she started to cry.

By this time, they were both upright and starting to look around the dimly lit mine shaft.

They both started to shout "Rich, Rich!"

"I think he must be back this way," said Ems. "He was behind us when the ceiling collapsed."

The girls started to crawl through the rubble, slowly moving the rocks, shouting Rich's name as they went. They had moved about six metres before they heard anything.

"Stop!" shouted Becks. They both stopped, waited and listened.

Finally, there came the movement of a few stones from just up ahead. The girls started to move towards the sound, pausing every couple of feet. Eventually, they could see where it was coming from - there was an overturned mine carriage which was on its side - and there was a bundle of rocks blocking the opening.

"Rich, can you hear us?" shouted Ems.

More rubble moved and eventually they could hear Rich's voice through the stones. The girls quickly got to work uncovering the opening to the overturned carriage. They found Rich sitting inside it, not hurt in anyway as the carriage had protected him.

He crawled out and gave both the girls a hug, delighted that they had found him.

"I couldn't hear anything," said Rich. "There was just silence. I kept moving the rocks away but there was just so many in front of me I thought I was never going to get out. I did find this one though!"

Rich held up a rock that looked just like the first jigsaw rock. It had similar markings on it.

"Excellent!" squealed Becks, delighted. "How were you able to see?"

"I forgot I had a small torch on my watch. Let's get out of here now that we have it," said Rich.

At that moment there was an enormous explosion from beneath their feet.

"What on earth was that? Move quickly!" screamed Ems.

Within seconds they could see the problem. The water that they had seen from the level below was starting to rise through the shaft. The speed at which it was rising was unbelievable. Within a few seconds, the level they were standing on had started to fill up with water.

"We'd better move!" screamed Rich.

Just as he said that, there was a loud gushing sound behind them. He started to run to the entrance of the mineshaft. In seconds the water had gone from ankle level to above their knees. The next thing they knew, the water had struck them from behind. Torrents of water were flooding through the level. The children were swept away, their arms flailing as the water carried them down the passage, screaming and trying desperately to hold onto something. Rich managed to grab some rocks at the side and was able to pull himself up higher. He reached out a hand and grabbed Becks as she went past and dragged her up too. Ems, however, continued to be swept away, Rich and Becks both screaming after her. Ems continued for another few metres, reaching out, desperate to find something to hold onto. She was eventually stopped abruptly by a pile of rocks that were in the way. Ems hit them with such a force that she screamed out in agony. She held on tightly, praying that the rocks wouldn't give way with the force of the water.

After another couple of minutes, the water gradually started to subside. The torrent turned to a gush, which turned into a trickle.

"Ems, are you okay?" shouted Rich from further up the shaft.

"I'm okay!" yelled back Ems.

They waded through the water, which was now knee deep, to get to her. Ems had a large hole in her trousers and a big gash on her leg which was bleeding.

"We'll need to get that looked at when we get out of here," said Becks.

Rich put his arm around Ems, and she hobbled with his assistance through the passageway to the bottom of steps going up to the next level. It took a few minutes for them to get Ems up the stairs. There was no one to be seen - they had probably all gone up to the safety of ground level when they heard the explosions. They made their way wearily along to the lift, starting to feel cold and shivery since they were soaked through.

They ascended to the ground level and as they got out the lift lots of people surrounded them. Ems, Rich and Becks were taken into the first aid room nearby and were checked over by a kind man and woman. Rich took the two rocks out of his pocket and put them down safely. Ems had her wound cleaned and a dressing and bandage applied, and they all got the chance to put on some dry clothes while their own ones were washed. Rich and Becks were very lucky, they just had some minor cuts and bruises. After they had a hot drink and a bit of a rest, the woman said they had a visitor.

Palesa came in the door saying, "I'm so glad you are okay. I was so worried when the explosion happened and you didn't appear. I said to Marge (pointing to the kind lady) that you're part of the school class and that our teacher has informed your parents. I think you had better slip out when they're not looking, because if they ask my teacher, they'll realise that you shouldn't have been here, and you might end up in a bit of bother."

"Thanks, Palesa. You've been a great friend. We know which school you're at, so we'll contact you when we're home," said Becks, looking sad.

"I hope you find what you're searching for. I can't wait to hear from you," said Palesa as she gave her new friends a hug goodbye. She waved and then disappeared out the door.

The three children quickly gathered up their clean but damp clothes and the two rocks, and when the adults weren't looking, quickly left the first aid station.

"Let's find a quiet space and have a good look at the map again. At least we have two rocks now," said Rich, looking pleased with himself. "We'll need a bag for them soon though, if we get any more!

Chapter 9

Ems, Rich and Becks soon found an area where they wouldn't be disturbed, underneath one of the park's roller coasters. Every few minutes the clickety clack of the roller coaster carriages would be heard noisily above them, and then they would hear the screams of enjoyment coming from the riders.

They looked at the map and the next area they were to travel to was Kruger National Park.

"It's huge!" said Becks, studying the map. "It looks like it's in the area near Satara Rest Camp."

"Let's go then," said Ems.

They all put their fingers on the map and said, "Kruger National Park."

Like before, they found themselves whirling and spinning as they made their way to Kruger. Landing more softly than previously, they managed a roll before stopping.

"Ouch!" screamed Ems, looking at her bandaged leg.

"You'll need to be careful you don't knock it," said Rich. "It isn't bleeding through the bandage though, so hopefully it will be alright for a while."

They looked around where they were and realised that they were actually in the rest camp. Lots of small buildings were dotted around, with signs for the shop and restaurant. It was starting to get dark and a bit colder too.

"Let's see if any of these bungalows are empty and see if we can try to get some sleep," said Becks.

They looked in a few of them until they came across one that was empty and open. In they went and before long they were all fast asleep.

Night fell. As the three children slept soundly, the sounds of roaring, whistling, chirping, bellowing and grunting could be heard outside, but still they slept, worn out by the day's events.

Ems woke up first and quietly went over to the window to look out. She gasped as she saw a giraffe in the distance strutting around. Ems knew that giraffes are browsers, as they eat the leaves and shoots from the trees and shrubs, rather than grazers which eat the grass.

After a few moments just watching the giraffe quietly herself, she decided to wake the others. Rich and Becks came and joined her outside just as the day was dawning.

"Wow! I can't believe we're on safari! All the animals I have dreamt of seeing and they are all actually here!" Ems said excitedly. "Let's see if we can find some of them before we try to find the rock."

"Since we're here, it seems a waste not to," said Rich, nodding his head in agreement.

With that, the three children got ready for the day ahead. They left the bungalow and went out to investigate the rest camp. Quickly they realised that you don't just walk through the National Park, you had to be in a vehicle. Any walks were with armed guides.

"This is going to be a problem if we need to get on an organised tour," voiced Becks.

"Let's watch the tour vehicles for a bit and see what happens," answered Rich, looking optimistic.

Within minutes, they managed to get on one of the larger jeeps. There appeared to be a few seats available and when the guide was distracted chatting to someone, they got on, took one of the park maps and sat towards the back.

"Welcome, my name is Lethabo and I'm going to be taking you into the wilderness that is Kruger National Park. Your driver's name is Junior and he's hoping that there will be plenty for you to see today," said Lethabo.

After going over some safety tips, the jeep left the rest camp. Some of the roads were paved, but it was still a bumpy ride at times.

The vast wilderness of the park passed them - extensive grasslands, mixed woodlands and many species of trees. After just a few minutes of driving, they stopped to watch a giraffe at the side of the road. The graceful mammal was eating from an acacia tree. Lethabo announced that it was a lone male giraffe, and was average in height for a male, about five metres tall. Its long purple tongue can grasp well which means it can strip a branch of the leaves and avoid the thorns. They moved on and stopped several times with Lethabo explaining what animal they were seeing - striped zebras in their family groups, vultures in trees awaiting a carcass for their next meal, a migratory herd of wildebeest and numerous sightings of different species of antelope.

Lethabo explained that the impala was the most common antelope with the kudu being the next common.

"Here's a wee rhyme that I love. If you could do what a kudu could do, you could be a kudu too," said Lethabo with a laugh.

The children continued to gaze in wonder at the amazing sights that were passing before their eyes as they drove through this vast savannah.

"Look over there," said Becks, pointing at a herd of buffalo in the distance all sitting in the shade under a group of trees.

"This is just out of this world," whispered Ems, in awe at all that she could see. "It's just a dream come true!"

Chapter 10

Suddenly, out of nowhere, a black-robed figure appeared in front of the jeep causing Junior to swerve to avoid it. The jeep left the road and hit some dried mud at the side which unbalanced it, then careered down a slope, with the passengers screaming and clinging onto the seat in front. Junior struggled to keep control of the vehicle and eventually hit a tree, stopping with a huge jolt. Everyone in the jeep was shaken and had minor bumps, but there were no serious injuries.

Ems, Becks and Rich clambered out from the back of the jeep, making sure everyone was okay.

Junior had a look at the jeep's engine which by now was open with steam hissing from it.

"Everyone gather round," said Lethabo. "Are you all okay? I have a first aid kit here if anyone needs anything."

All the passengers from the jeep nodded that they were fine. A few looked a bit ashen-faced and shaken from the experience.

Junior came over and updated everyone with the status of the vehicle.

"I'm afraid that the jeep is beyond repair now. There is too much damage to the front, and I can't get access to it as the tree is in the way. Lethabo has contacted the park security and they are sending help as we speak," said Junior.

"If we can all make our way to that group of trees over there, we will hopefully be safe sheltering there. Please be quiet as we don't want to alert some animals to our presence," added Lethabo.

Everyone picked up their belongings and started to walk over to the trees. A voice rang out over the group.

"I have caught up with you now," said this rasping voice. "I have waited years for someone to complete the jigsaw as you did and to be transported by the portal to one of the countries. I can't let you finish the puzzle and let the magic out. At least if I finish you off the others can remain sleeping and not be awoken."

Rich looked about, unable to see where the voice was coming from.

"It's the same voice as before," whimpered Becks, visibly shaking. "What are we going to do?"

"It will find us if we stay here," said Ems. "We need to go now. We don't know what it's going to do to us - but it doesn't sound good!"

The three children quickly took to their heels and ran to the trees with the rest of the group but once they got there, they kept on going. They ran a bit further, and then stopped and looked back from the cover of a bush. In the distance they could see the figure approach the group, looking carefully at them all before an awful scream came from it.

"Where are you? There is no escaping me!" the figure screamed as it looked around hungrily.

They could see it sniffing the air as if trying to get a trace of them.

"Wait till it looks the other way and then we need to run," whispered Rich to the others.

A few seconds later, he gave Ems and Becks a nudge and they started to run in a straight line with the large bush giving them cover. They ran solidly for five minutes, Becks encouraging the others quietly, as she was barely out of breath. Rich by now was looking very red-faced and hot and bothered. Ems was a bit out of breath too but was still managing a slight jog. They came to a stop when they realised that the wooded area was coming to an end. Stopping at the edge of it, they looked out at the vast, open area in front of them. There was the occasional bush and some large rocks dotted about, but largely it was just grass and lots of it.

"What do we do now?" gasped Ems as she breathed heavily.

"Let's have a quick look at the map of the park and try to see where we are, and then try to match that with where the next clue and rock are on our map" said Rich, huffing and puffing. He took both the maps out of the bag and looked at them side by side. They could see where the rest camp was on the map and a few areas that they had passed which Lethabo had pointed out

– the waterhole, the junction of two roads, the dried-up river bed.

"It looks like we're somewhere about here," Rich said, circling a rather large area on the map. "And this is where we need to get to."

He pointed to a small river which had a ford going over it.

"I think the rock will be there somewhere" he said. "We need to head in that direction. We're about two or three miles away, I would think."

"Two or three miles? Walking in this?" exclaimed Becks, looking worried. "We're on the African plains, not walking through our local park." Her voice started to get higher as she said it.

"Well, we have two choices. We either stay here and wait for that thing to find us or we try to find a way out of here. I'm prepared to take a chance to try and get a bit closer to home," said Ems.

Reluctantly, Becks agreed. Rich, consulting the map one last time, pointed in the direction that they should be headed in.

"Let's try to be quiet, only talking when we need to - and keep an eye out at all times both in front and behind. We should walk in a line. Ems, you go at the front, Becks you go in the middle, and I'll keep a look about behind," said Rich.

The children started to walk through the dried grassy plain, all avidly looking around them for any signs of movement. They slowly walked past a group of zebras just grazing, eyeing them carefully as they went by. After a few minutes, they all began to relax a bit, as they were enjoying the walk through the beautiful scenery. Where the ground was muddy, they pointed out tracks in silence to each other – different sizes of footprints all belonging to various animals and birds. Some of the rocks were huge and they had to go around these, all the time looking and listening.

After about twenty minutes, Rich signalled to stop behind the next large rock and brought out the maps, just to check they were heading in the right direction. In the distance, they saw a road. They heard the sound of jeeps getting louder as they neared, on their way to pick up Lethabo, Junior and the rest of the group. They hid behind the rock, not wanting to be seen as they were so close to finding the next piece of the puzzle.

Once the jeeps had gone past, they changed direction and walked along parallel to the road for a time. Suddenly, there seemed to be a change in the noises around them.

A strange kind of laughing started. They stopped still. Listening. Looking. Squealing noises and groaning sounds and then a funny whoop.

Em's face changed to anguish. She whispered, "That's the sound of hyenas!"

They quickly walked silently to the shelter of the next bush and crouched behind it. From there they could see a pack of hyenas coming towards them, the dominant female at the front. There were about fifteen in the pack, with at least four smaller hyenas. With a sloping back and coarse, spotted fur, Ems soon identified them as spotted hyenas.

The children held their breath as the pack got closer and closer. The female at the front suddenly stopped. It sniffed the air and made a whooping noise. Within seconds, another whooping sound was heard from a distance and then the laugh again. The female made a noise to the rest of the pack, and they about turned and headed in the direction of the laugh. Peering through the bush, the children could make out in the distance some vultures circling and also some activity on the ground. Ems with her sharp eyes could see there was an animal on the ground and a small pack of hyenas feeding. The other pack soon reached the feast that was on offer. Fighting quickly ensued amongst the hyenas as they all tried to get in a prime position to eat, the vultures above swooping in every now and then to try to pick up some scraps.

While this was going on, Ems signalled to the others to leave the shelter of the bush and make their way around the pack at some distance quickly and quietly. This meant that they had a large detour to make to avoid being seen. Fortunately, the hyenas were too busy feasting to be aware of the children passing.

They walked silently for another ten minutes until they were well away from the hyenas and then they stopped and were able to speak quietly.

"That was awful," said Becks. "I thought they'd seen us."

"The hyenas maybe knew we were there, but they probably thought that it was easier to go to the animal that had already been caught, than trying to hunt us," said Rich. He brought the map out again and tried to see where they were.

"If we manage to find this river," he explained, pointing to the map. "We can follow it along till we come to the ford."

They got back in formation again and started to walk, all looking and listening for the sound of water. Giraffes in the distance, ignoring them as they went by, birds cheeping around them and a rustling noise as the gentle breeze went through the long grasses. At last, they could hear the faint sound of water and walked quickly towards it. They were relieved when they saw the winding, fast flowing river in front of them. Looking both ways they tried to see if they could spot the ford.

"Which way do you reckon we go?" asked Becks.

"I think we will just need to pick one and hope for the best," replied Rich. "Let's go left."

Chapter 11

The children walked along the muddy riverbank, careful not to go anywhere near the edge. On the other side of the river, they could see some large rocks, but Rich pointed out they were not rocks, but hippopotamuses wallowing in the water.

One of them suddenly opened its massive jaws and the children could see, even from where they were standing, its enormous teeth. Another hippo had approached it and was baring its teeth, probably because it felt threatened.

They watched these magnificent creatures for a few minutes before they realised that on the riverbank opposite were some crocodiles catching the sun. Looking quickly on their side, the children breathed a sigh of relief as they couldn't see any danger ahead.

Walking again, they made their way along, noticing some tracks in the mud made by numerous animals and birds.

After walking for another fifteen minutes, they could see that the river had become a little narrower and they were just hoping that the crossing they were looking for was ahead. They were about twenty metres from the crossing when there came an almighty noise. The group froze. A herd of wildebeest came thundering just in front of them. Hundreds of them, all different sizes, came down from the grasslands and into the river.

Becks, Ems and Rich all watched in wonder as the herd ran through the water. Only then did they notice why the wildebeest were running. A pride of lions was running amongst them, trying to separate the smaller or older wildebeest.

The children quickly ran and hid behind a tree, watching, mesmerized by the scene in front of them. They then realised that there was an even bigger threat. In the perilous waters of the river, the sleepy crocodiles were now awake and were now trying to bite and drown the more vulnerable wildebeest.

Minutes went by as hundreds of wildebeest crossed the river, risking their lives, trying to avoid the lions and the crocodiles. Unfortunately, some were unlucky, drowned by the crocodiles and dragged to the land to be devoured later. Others were attacked by the lions, killed and dragged away for the lions to feast upon.

Lastly, some wildebeest slipped and were pushed and trampled on by some of their own herd. It made for dismal viewing, but the children found it was fascinating at the same time to witness this part of the circle of life.

Eventually, the herd of wildebeest passed and all that was left were the cries of the fallen ones being attacked by their lion or crocodile hunters. The children waited for a couple of hours until bodies had been dragged away and they felt that the area in front was clear of any predators. They cautiously wandered along the riverside, looking around them as they went.

When they got to the ford, they looked for rocks. There were none on the crossing as it was basically cement. However, at each end of the ford there was a border of rocks. The children quickly got to work looking at the nearest border. Most of them were huge and not like the ones that they were looking for. They examined one side of the crossing before jogging to the other side to look at the rocks there. Busily investigating them, they were unaware of a predator approaching. Hearing a noise, Ems looked up.

"Don't move!" she whispered, standing as still as a statue.

The others froze and moved their eyes towards where Ems was looking. A sharp intake of breath was heard as Becks saw what was there.

A lioness was moving slowly through the grass about fifteen metres from where they were. Becks moved her eyes and looked down at the rock at her feet.

"I've found the rock," she said in a whisper, her lips barely moving. All this time the lioness was getting closer and closer.

"On the count of three, Becks, pick up the rock, put it on the ground. All three of us put one finger on it and say Addo Elephant," said Ems.

Without waiting for any response from the other two, Ems said, "One, two, three." The children all moved in unison.

Aware of their movement, the lioness was now running towards them at a frightening speed.

After Ems had counted to three, the rock was on the ground and placing their fingers on it they shouted, "Addo Elephant!"

The last thing that they saw before hurtling towards their next location was the lioness leaping through the air, teeth bared ready to attack them.

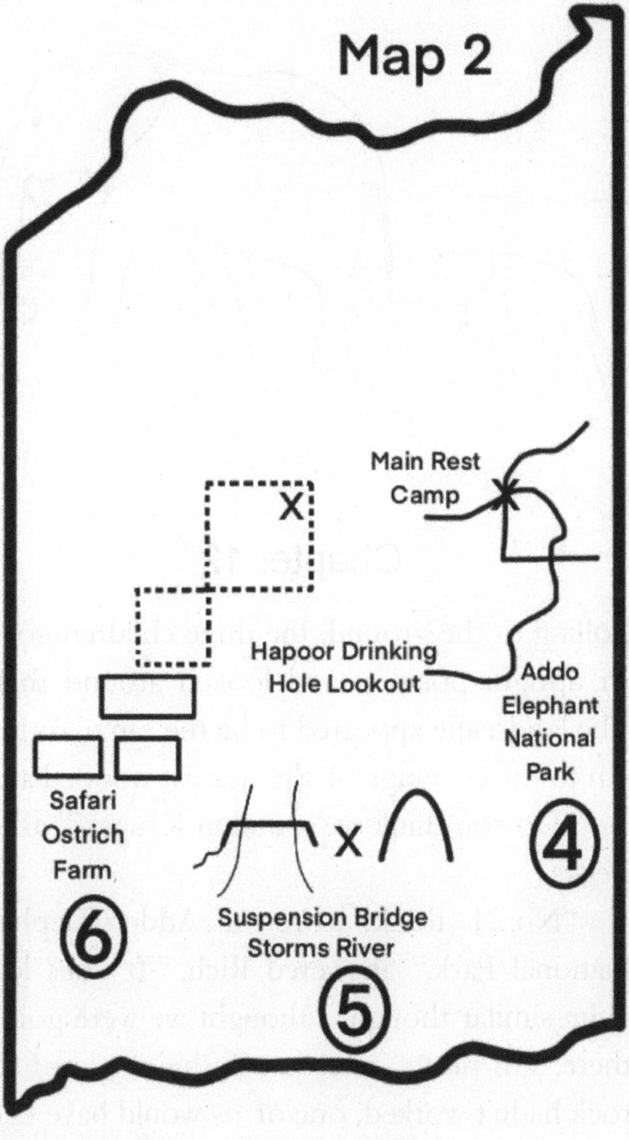
Map 2
Main Rest
Camp
X
Hapoor Drinking
Hole Lookout
Addo
Elephant
National
Park
4
Safari
Ostrich
Farm
6
X
Suspension Bridge
Storms River
5

Chapter 12

Rolling to the ground, the three children got in an upright position and looked around them. The landscape appeared to be the same, so they ran to the coverage of the nearest wooded area.

"Do you think we're still in Kruger?" asked Becks.

"No, I think we're in Addo Elephant National Park," answered Rich. "It does look quite similar though. I thought we were goners there. I'm pretty sure that if the magic of the rock hadn't worked, one of us would have been mauled to death."

The two girls nodded and sank to the ground in relief.

"That was so lucky you found the rock when you did," said Ems to Becks.

"I hadn't found it before you saw the lioness, but when I looked down, I saw it had the markings on it," she said.

They all sat on the ground for the next few minutes trying to come to terms with what had just happened.

Eventually, Ems got to her feet and said that they had better find shelter for the night as the sun was getting lower in the sky. Standing up, they looked around at their surroundings. In the distance they could see a lone adult male elephant walking, but it was too far away to be bothered by them.

"What about over there?" pointed Becks, looking at a small thicket. They all headed over and before long had found an area that was quite secluded and sheltered. Becks managed to put together a makeshift bed using grass to make it a bit softer, and then using some loose, large branches she made a basic shelter.

"Wow," said Rich, looking impressed. "Where did you learn to make that?"

"I'm in the Girl Guides and have been camping before. We took part in a challenge when we were away to make a shelter using natural materials. Hopefully it will give us a bit of shelter tonight if it does rain and will keep us a bit warmer," said Becks, feeling delighted with herself.

By this time, the sun was very low in the sky. The children watched it for a few minutes, in awe at the beauty. Different shades of yellow, orange and red adorned the sky as the sun gradually disappeared.

At this, the three children went into their makeshift shelter and lay together on the ground. They were soon asleep, dreaming of the sunset, the animals they had encountered and of home.

In the middle of the night, they were awoken by the sound of large rain drops. Fortunately for them, there were just a couple of small areas that were leaking and Becks soon filled them in with leaves.

The children went back to sleep, confident that the shelter would withstand the rain. It stopped about an hour later and as dawn broke, the children slept on.

Ems woke first, content to lie and listen to the noises nearby, as she checked that the dressing on her leg was still secure. The morning sounds were different to those that were heard in the evening. Animals were stirring and birds were flying around looking for food and twigs for their nests.

It wasn't long before the other children awoke, and they too enjoyed listening to the sounds of the park waking up. Rich brought out the map and had a look at it.

"We need to find out exactly where we are first," he said.

They all got to their feet and started walking through the thicket. From the edge of the thicket, they could see a large adult male elephant in the distance just minding its own business. They walked in the other direction so as not to disturb it, looking around at the landscape trying to find some clue to discover their location.

Before long, they came across a mother elephant and a calf in the distance. Sitting quietly on the ground, the three children observed them from afar. The calf was staying very close to the mother, who was very nurturing towards it. It was using its trunk in a sweeping movement to gather grass and leaves in a pile and then crushing them to a solid state so that it could then pick it up with its trunk to eat. It was amazing watching these fantastic creatures and observing them in real life in the wild. The calf, which always stayed in close proximity to the mother, decided quite quickly that it was very hungry so went to the mother to feed. Watching this endearing moment brought a tear to the children's eyes.

Reluctantly, they got up and started to walk again, quickly coming to a dirt road. They were able to follow this for a few minutes until they heard the noise of a car. Looking around for somewhere to hide, they found a ditch near the side of the road. The car passed slowly with a family of four in it, looking out with their binoculars trying to spot elephants. Once the car was out of sight, the children continued to follow the road.

Within minutes, they were at a large watering hole. There were some bushes around one end, so the children hid themselves there to observe what was going on. There were a couple of cars at the watering hole, their passengers eagerly watching the scene before them. A herd of about fourteen elephants, were already there drinking the water using their trunks like a straw to suck the water up and then squirting the water into their mouth. Some were spraying the water over themselves to cool off. Several were female elephants, and the rest were calves of varying ages. Two of the bigger male calves, started to confront each other. They used their small growing tusks as a defence mechanism, each trying to battle for dominance.

The children watched, their mouths agape at the spectacle of the fight. The people in the cars also watched it, although at one point the duelling elephants came quite close to them. Eventually, exhausted from all the fighting back and forward, the pair gave up and went their separate ways. The herd soon all moved away.

"Look!" exclaimed Becks. "Another herd!"

Ems and Rich looked and, sure enough, another herd was just arriving from the hill beyond the waterhole. In the distance, behind them, was another herd.

"Wow, this is amazing!" said Ems excitedly. "There are so many of them."

After another five minutes, the herd had arrived at the waterhole and took their turn at drinking, playing and cooling down. A lone male also arrived and ignored the other elephants. Some of the young elephants were playing - bumping and chasing each other.

The only time the male elephant bothered about them was when they got too near. He then trumpeted to let them know to go away.

"The calves are so cute playing around," cooed Ems. "I wish I had a camera or phone to take photos or videos of them."

They spent the next hour observing the elephants coming and going from the waterhole. It was the most amazing sight.

When the last of the herds had left the waterhole, Rich got out the map and had a good look at it.

"I can see where we are," he said. "We've got to walk a bit further through the park to get to where the next portal is. If we continue to follow this road, we should get there quite quickly."

They got to their feet and started to walk, far enough away from the road to be able to hide if a car appeared, passing various types of antelope – eland, kudu, and impala - and buffalo.

While they were walking, they talked about the black hooded figure and the message it had given them.

"Who do you suppose the others are?" asked Becks. "What do you think it meant when it said that it had waited years for someone to finish the jigsaw, as we did?"

"I've been wondering about that too," said Rich. "I think it might be about the way we completed the puzzle. Who put the last piece in?"

"I did - and it was a South Africa piece!" gasped Ems, just realising the link.

"I think we need to keep going until we find all the pieces of the puzzle and get home, and hopefully that will be the end of it," said Becks. "We can look in the library when - or if - we get back and see what any of this has to do with your new house, Ems."

"I wonder who the others are though?" said Ems, shrugging.

"I think I'd rather not find out," said Becks with a shudder.

They passed a tree, and it was only as they went under it that they realised that there was a tail hanging down from it.

"Ssh," whispered Ems, pointing upwards.

There, about two metres above them, was a leopard draped over a branch. It appeared to be sleeping, but the three children were taking no chances and quickly hurried onwards as quietly as they could.

Chapter 13

At this point, the children entered an area of trees and shrubs.

"The portal should just be on the other side of this area," said Rich, inspecting the map quickly. "It's on the corner where two of the roads meet just before you come to the rest camp."

It was quite a dense area, so they had to push back some of the branches to get past. Suddenly, there was a loud noise. The children all looked around, struggling to see anything through the thick wall of shrubs and bushes. Then came another sound. The children couldn't place what it was, and then out of nowhere, an enormous elephant came running at them. They all screamed with fright and flung themselves on the ground out of its path. They could hear more branches snapping and feet thundering.

"Move!" shouted Rich.

The children all got up and started to run, looking for somewhere to find some cover. A couple of smaller elephants overtook them. The children ran as fast as they could getting scratched by the branches and thorns and using their hands to shield their eyes and to move anything getting in the way. Ems moved over to the right a bit as she'd spotted a tree. She stood directly behind the trunk, praying that it was sturdy enough that the herd would just pass by it rather than try to run at it.

The elephants ran past her at speed, but they moved to avoid the tree, and none tried to push the tree down. She glanced around to see where Becks and Rich had gone.

Becks had seen another tree in the distance. Being a fast runner, she had sprinted to it, trying to zig zag out of the way of any large bushes to avoid the elephants that were starting to overtake her. Mother elephants with their older calves were running through, making it difficult for her to see what was ahead. When she got to the tree she jumped, managing to grab hold of a branch which she swung back and forward on a couple of times before getting enough momentum to swing herself up into the tree. From there, she was quite safe as the tree was huge and the elephants were avoiding any large obstacles in the way. She had a bird's eye view from there and could see Ems standing still behind the tree, and the elephants continuing to pass her in a rush.

Becks looked around for Rich, but he was nowhere to be seen.

Meanwhile, Rich, not being particularly fast, had fallen behind and had eventually tripped over a branch that was on the ground. He curled up and tried to protect his head as the elephants charged by. He knew that if the elephants didn't find you a threat, then they probably wouldn't trample you. However, the elephants were so spooked by whatever had startled them that they weren't really paying attention to where they were running. They were just getting away from the threat that was posed. Rich rolled and moved position a couple of times to try and get out of the main path. By now it was the slower elephants going by - the older ones and the mother elephants with the small calves. Rich had just moved when he felt an almighty pain on his thigh. One of the young calves had placed their foot on him as they were running. He gave out an almighty yelp and curled up even more, nursing his sore leg.

Eventually, the herd passed. Becks could see from the top of the tree that there were no more elephants, but she still couldn't see what had frightened them. She waited another couple of minutes just to be sure and then climbed down the tree, making her way over to where Ems was still standing behind the tree trunk.

"I'm so pleased to see you," said Ems, giving her a hug. "I didn't know where you both had gone. I thought the herd was never going to pass."

"I went up that tree over there," said Becks. "But I have no idea where Rich went."

The girls started to move through the area calling his name. It was easier now to move, as so many of the bushes and shrubs had been flattened by the elephants. After a couple of minutes, they heard a voice shouting to them. They ran over and there was Rich clutching his thigh. He was examining his injury. It was red looking and would probably turn into a colourful bruise as it healed. He was lucky that it had been one of the smaller elephant calves, as one of the larger ones would have probably broken his leg.

"I'm okay," he said, still investigating his injury. "I thought I was going to be completely trampled. It's sore, but I think it will only be bruised. I wonder what spooked them?"

With the help of Ems and Becks at either side of him, Rich got to his feet. Once standing, he started to walk and seemed to manage well enough, although it would be tender to touch for the next few days.

The three of them followed in the footsteps of the herd through the trampled vegetation to the other side of the thicket. They could see the elephants in the distance now all just walking.

"There's the crossroads over there," said Becks excitedly to the others.

They all started to walk over. Fortunately for them there weren't many rocks about. After looking at two rocks, Ems shouted over that she had found the jigsaw piece.

"This place was amazing," said Ems. "Just a pity that the elephant stampede had to spoil it."

Rich got out the map again. "The next place is Storms River," he said.

They all placed their fingers on the rock and shouted, "Storms River." Immediately, they were spinning and turning on their way there.

Chapter 14

Landing, still rolling but managing to get to their feet more quickly, they were now mastering the art of portal travelling.

"Before long we'll be landing on our feet," said Becks.

"Well, you might, but I don't think there's any chance I'll be doing that," said Rich with a smile. He knew his limits, and landing gracefully was probably not going to be one of them.

"No, I expect you're right," laughed the girls.

The children had a look around them and realised that they were just beside a picnic site with fantastic views of the ocean. They went over and looked at the waves breaking on the rocks. Next to that there were some people getting ready to go kayaking.

There was also a map in the picnic area. Rich took his map out and they walked over to the noticeboard. Comparing both the maps, he could see where they were going to have to walk to get to the next portal.

"We're here," he said, pointing to the map on the noticeboard. "If we follow this path, it will take us to Storms River Mouth and then we can cross the bridge there. The rock should be somewhere just over the other side before you start to climb that hill."

They looked over past the map, and in the distance, not too far away, was the hill that was on the map. At that moment, a woman came over.

"Hi, I was just wondering if you would like the leftovers from our picnic. We brought far too much food, and it's just going to go to waste as we're going to a friend's house tonight for dinner."

"That would be great!" said Rich enthusiastically. "Thank you so much. We were going to have to find something to eat."

With that, the woman about turned and picked up the empty picnic bag that was on the table. Her family all waved, and the three children shouted over, "thank you," as they left.

The children sat down at the table, which still looked pretty full of food and bottles of water. There were the remnants of the braai, or barbecue, that the family had just finished eating. The children tucked into the food – chicken legs, burgers, rolls, cheese – it was absolute heaven.

"Maybe we should keep some for later," said Becks.

"Absolutely," said Rich, talking with his mouth full.

Ems and Becks started to pack the savoury food and bottles of water in a bag that had been left, as Rich started to investigate the sweet treats. They had one small cake each and put the rest in the bag.

While they were finishing off, they realised that there was a rodent-like animal about the size of a small dog near them. Looking around, they saw that there were a few of them. They seemed quite tame and appeared to be eating any food that people had dropped on the ground.

Ems, who knew a lot about animals, was a bit perplexed.

"I'm really not sure what these are. I'm going to ask someone."

She went over to the people getting the kayaks ready and asked them. A couple of minutes later she came back and filled Becks and Rich in.

"They are mammals called dassies. They are found in rocky places and eat mainly plants, although they do like some food remains. Funny fact though - they are apparently related to the elephant."

"The elephant!" said Becks, looking at the dassies around them. "They don't look anything like them."

"They are the closest living relative of the African elephant, despite the difference in size. They have a similar structure in their feet and teeth through evolution."

"That's amazing!" said Rich. "I can't wait to get home and look all this up on the internet."

Gathering up the bag of food and putting the rocks inside it - as Rich's pockets were now starting to look rather full - they made their way to the path at the start of the trail. After a few minutes of walking and going up steps through the forest, they came across a viewpoint. It offered fantastic views of the ocean. Continuing on their way, they found some paths that detoured to some small, picturesque beaches.

The children stopped for a while to take in the view. It was so peaceful. The water breaking on the rocks was just mesmerising. Other than that, they could hear no other sound, except for the occasional bird chirping. They lay down in the sun, enjoying the warmth.

After an hour, they got to their feet and made their way back up to the path. From the path they could see the bridge. Shortly after, they arrived at Storms River Mouth and the suspension bridge.

They climbed down to the bridge using the steps. There was nobody on it at that moment, but they could see other people making their way up the hill on the other side.

"It said on the map that this bridge is seventy-seven metres long and about seven metres above the water," said Rich.

Becks stepped on the bridge first.

"It's like the wee bridges you get in play parks back home," she said. "It does move about quite a lot though."

Ems and Rich made their way on to the bridge. It certainly did bounce when they walked along it. Ems wasn't too sure if she liked it much. She was slightly scared of piers or bridges with slats, as she didn't like looking through them to see the water underneath.

"Will you two stop bouncing! You know I don't like anything where there are wooden slats and water," Ems said in an anxious voice.

By this time, they had reached the middle of the bridge and were looking at the views. Looking out to where the river mouth meets the Indian Ocean, the waves from the ocean were breaking upon the water from the river, creating some strong currents.

Looking the other way, the children could see a group of kayakers making their way down the river. The group were easy to spot in their brightly coloured kayaks and life jackets. Cliffs surrounded them on each side.

Ems still looked nervous as they started to make their way to the other side of the bridge. A strong wind was now blowing which added to the thrill for the other two but had Ems almost crying as she clung onto the side of the bridge, pulling herself along.

They weren't far from the end when the children heard a noise from behind them. They turned around and there was the hooded, black figure at the opposite end of the bridge! The children stood stunned, legs unable to move, as the figure came towards them.

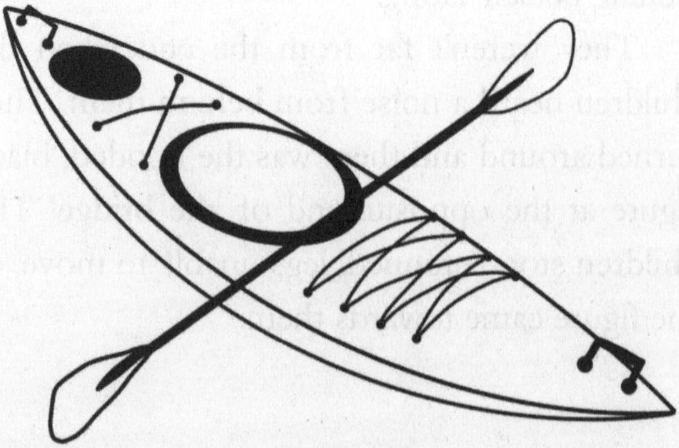

Chapter 15

“Did you think you could escape? You were lucky to get out of the jeep in Kruger, but I can’t let you complete the jigsaw,” the figure shouted.

“Why don’t you want us to get back home?” whimpered Becks.

“If you get back home, a part of Michael comes alive again, and I will disappear forever. I can’t let you do that,” it rasped.

“Who is Michael?” cried Ems.

They hadn’t seen its hands before and all shivered when the withered hands appeared with something that looked like a pair of sharp shears.

Before they could move, the figure had swung the shears round and had cut through one of the cables of the suspension bridge. The children screamed as they realised what was going to happen. Ems was still clinging on to the side railing and Becks and Rich grabbed onto it just in time as the other cable was cut. The black, hooded figure seemed to just disappear into thin air.

Within seconds, the other end of the bridge had collapsed into the river and the weight of it was dragging the rest of the bridge down. The children held on desperately, screaming, as slat by slat, the bridge tumbled into the water like a concertina.

The children screamed as they, and the part of the bridge on which they had been standing, disappeared under the water. Becks was the first to surface. Using the front crawl, she managed to swim up the river away from the churning waters ahead.

Ems was next to surface, and she seemed to have managed to keep a hold of the bridge and had been pulling herself along it. She was able to clamber up the slats like a ladder until she was at the other end of the bridge which was still intact. From there she could see Becks swimming across the river to the side. She was a strong swimmer as well as a great all round athlete.

Ems noticed that Rich had surfaced, taking a huge breath, but was struggling to swim against the flow of the river. He tried hard to use the front crawl, but any progress he made was quickly undone. Gradually, he was getting swept out of the calm river mouth into the Indian Ocean. Where the river and ocean met was a swirling, foamy, deadly strong current.

"Help!" he shouted, as he tried in vain to swim against the current.

"Hold on!" a voice shouted. Two of the kayakers who had been part of the group had paddled down the river when they saw the bridge collapse and were just metres away from where Rich was.

"Keep trying to swim towards us!" shouted a blonde-haired man. Rich was just treading water. For every half metre he moved forward he was pushed back about a metre, and so was being swept closer to the churning sea. The man had tied his kayak to his friend's kayak, and he was continuing to paddle against the current.

Meanwhile, the dark-haired woman had got a towline out of her kayak and was throwing the line towards Rich. After four attempts, during which Rich was getting dragged further away, he managed to catch it. The woman then pulled him through the water till he reached her kayak. She made a loop with the rope, put it round Rich's waist and tied it to the back of the kayak.

"Now, just relax and we're going to tow you over to the shore," the woman said. She got her paddle and started to propel the kayak with the man (who had untied the rope holding the two boats together) following behind to ensure that Rich didn't slip away.

Making slow progress against the current, they eventually got to a small pebble beach at the far end of the suspension bridge, where both Ems and Becks were waiting anxiously. The other kayakers had also stopped there and ran into the water to help them.

The man and woman got out of their kayaks and went to help Rich stand up. He was very tired after his exhausting swim. The group of eight kayakers couldn't have been nicer.

"Are you all okay?" the woman asked, introducing herself as Liv.

Both girls answered that they were okay, and Rich nodded his head. The group helped by looking in their back packs to get towels that they could wrap around the children, and they gave them some water. Ems quickly got up as she saw the bag that Rich had been carrying appear at the shoreline. When the bridge had collapsed, he had flung the bag as far as he could, to get it as near to the shore as possible. It had worked as it was all intact, although some of the food was probably soaked through.

The man, who said his name was Gus, used his radio to contact the nearby coastguard station.

"I have let them know that the bridge has collapsed and that three children have fallen into the water. They're going to send a boat along directly that will take you up the river where a first aider will assess you and take you to hospital if required."

"Thanks so much for all your help. Did you see the black, hooded figure on the bridge?" asked Ems.

"No, there was no one on the bridge apart from you three. Are you sure you're okay? It sounds like you might have hurt your head. There was definitely no one else," said Liv.

The others all nodded in agreement. Some of them went to sort out the kayaks. While they were busy, the three children started to chat.

"What are we going to do? We can't go in the boat. We are literally right here at the portal," said Becks.

"How are you feeling, Rich? We should go to the hospital if you're not feeling well. We can always come back another day," said Ems.

"I'm fine. I think I've nearly recovered now. I could do with a sleep though after all my swimming," replied Rich.

"Why don't we start to look around for the rock," said Ems to Becks. "And you sit here and try to recover. You could have a look in the food bag and see if there's anything we can salvage."

Rich emptied the bag and looked at everything. Some of the food would probably be inedible and could go straight into the bin but anything that was still in wrappers was fine. The rocks were still there too. One of the girls came over with a backpack.

"Look, have this to put all your things into," she said kindly.

Rich thanked her and put everything into it. She also gave Ems a new dressing for her leg to replace the now wet and grubby one. Fortunately, it was a warm day, and their clothes were drying in the sun.

A faint engine sound was heard in the distance. It was the boat coming closer.

"Becks, how are you getting on?" hissed Rich.

"Just got this last section to look at," Becks replied, looking quickly at the rocks.

The boat was moving closer and closer and getting noisier and noisier.

"Found it!" said Becks delighted, holding onto the small rock.

"You two girls quickly take the bag and go over beyond those bushes. I'll join you in a minute," said Rich.

He got up and went over to tell Gus he was just going to the toilet.

Gus nodded, "Be quick though, the boat's nearly here. They will check you over." He then turned back to the conversation he was having with some of the kayaking group.

Rich quickly walked over to behind the bushes where the girls were. As before, they put their fingers on the rock and said, "Safari Ostrich Farm," which was the next location on the map. The next minute they disappeared.

The group of kayakers hunted high and low, search parties were sent out, but no one ever discovered what happened to the three children.

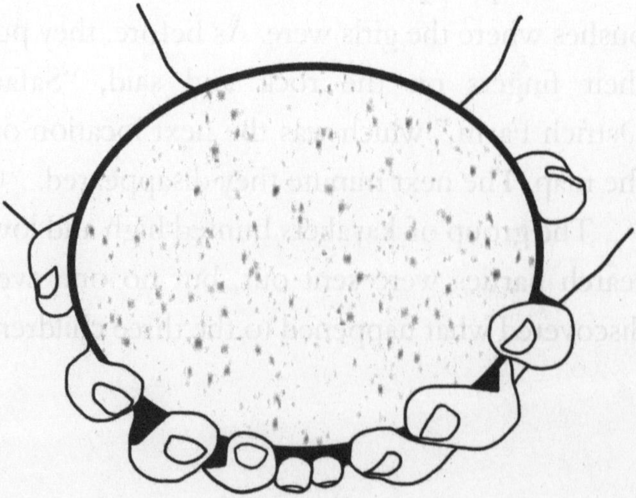

Chapter 16

Landing for the most part smoothly, the three children looked around at their surroundings. They seemed to be at some kind of farm, with large fences on every side and there were some buildings in the distance. There didn't seem to be anyone around, and certainly no animals that they could see.

Ems, Rich and Becks all sat down tired after their energetic swim in the river.

"How's your leg?" Ems asked Rich.

He pulled up his trousers to have a look. The bruise that he had got when the elephant trod on him was now a vivid purple colour covering quite a large area of his thigh.

"It's okay, it's not sore unless I touch it," he answered. He took out the map and had a look at it to see where the rock was located. Luckily, Rich was good at map-reading and working out directions. The girls would have been lost without him.

"The map shows that the rock is over there within one of the fenced fields," he said, pointing in the direction of the buildings and beyond them.

"It shouldn't take us too long to get there. I can't see anything that would stop us or slow us down. Hopefully this will be straightforward this time," said an optimistic Becks.

Ems started to move and the other two followed her. They got to the end of the field and clambered over the gate. By the time they reached the other end, they could see some movement in the distance.

"What's that?" said Ems, straining her eyes to get a better look. The other two had no chance of seeing it if Ems couldn't, she was very sharp-eyed. They all stared into the distance. "I think it might be ostriches. Thank goodness that's all it is."

By this time, they had reached the buildings and could see that there were some people walking around. There was a shop selling ostrich leather. Looking in the window they could see handbags, belts and wallets made from the leather. There were also ostrich eggs to use as ornaments which had been beautifully hand crafted and feather products like dusters.

Next to this was a restaurant. On the menu was an assortment of dishes, many of which used ostrich meat – burgers, wraps and soup. They all looked delicious.

The children joined a group that were with a tour guide. In one room there were incubators with eggs in them, and a few of them had babies that were trying to hatch out. They saw a man engraving the eggs and saw the leather up close. The man explained that the leather goes through a process of dyeing to provide all the contrasts of colour for the merchandise in the shop. The leather is unique in that it has spots all over it where the feathers grow.

Outside, the children took turns standing on top of an ostrich egg. Ems couldn't believe how large and strong it was. They stood on two eggs, the eggs taking their entire weight. Next, they fed the ostriches by taking the dried feed from the troughs with a spoon. They boarded the tractor with the group and went round the ostrich farm. Going through the gates into the field, the ostriches soon came over to the tractor and were running alongside it. Ems, Rich and Becks all made sure their arms were kept inside the trailer. The big ostrich beaks looked menacing as they kept pace with the tractor. They could see how fast the birds were as they ran past them. Ems was able to tell the others that the top speed ostriches can run is seventy kilometres per hour.

"Wow, that's so fast," said Becks, impressed with this statistic. "I wish I could run as fast as that."

"You're a really fast runner," said Ems kindly. "You win loads of races, and you compete in lots of competitions now. I'm sure one day you'll be at the Olympics."

Becks was really delighted with this praise from her friend.

While they were on the tractor, Rich took out the map to see exactly where the rock was.

It was in the field next to the one they were in. When the tractor got back to the buildings, the children got out, pleased to have experienced an ostrich farm and to have seen up close just how big ostriches are.

As soon as the others from the tractor had disappeared round the corner, the three children walked in the opposite direction. They followed much of the route the tractor had taken and found themselves in the same enclosure as before. Prior to making their way across, they made sure the ostriches were occupied at the other end. Quietly, they walked through it to the next field. Seeing nothing in the field, they climbed over the gate. They quickly looked around, noting that much of the field was barren. A few trees were dotted about around the sides to offer the ostriches some shelter from the weather, and there were some shrubs and succulent plants around.

"It shouldn't take too long to find the rock as there's not much in here," said Rich, scanning the field.

They walked over to the group of trees in the distance and started to look around them.

There was the odd small stone, but nothing big enough to have a part of the map on it. Working their way down the side of the field, they soon reached the bottom.

"Well, we've looked at half of the field now. Let's try the other side and then move to the shrubs that are dotted about," Ems suggested to the others.

The other two agreed, so they continued looking for about an hour, without success. There was just no sign of it anywhere. By this time, it was starting to get dark. Having one last look around, they decided to stop for the night.

"Will we try to go back to the buildings?" asked Becks. "Or would it be better to just stay here?"

"I think we should just stay here," answered Rich. "It means we can get an early start tomorrow and we are not worrying about people finding us."

"I agree," nodded Ems. "I'm a bit worried though. What if we don't find the stone? What happens to us? Can we say to the police that we're lost, and they will take us back home?"

"I was thinking about that too. That awful, hooded person would be glad if we didn't find all the pieces, but I'm not sure what the consequences are for us if we don't. It did warn us not to speak to anyone about it," said Becks, starting to look a bit worried.

"I'm sure we'll find it tomorrow," replied Ems, looking more optimistic as she realised that saying what she did had caused Becks to look even more worried. Becks was a bit of a worrier at times, but she did find taking part in all her sports made her feel better. Breathing in the air outside and getting her heart rate going, really made Becks feel like she could accomplish anything.

Making their way over to a couple of trees that were close together with a shrub in between them made a perfect shelter for them. They put their jumpers on as it would be sure to become colder overnight. Eating a small meal but being careful to leave some food for the next day, they enjoyed what they ate. Still tired after their swim earlier, they quickly drifted off to sleep.

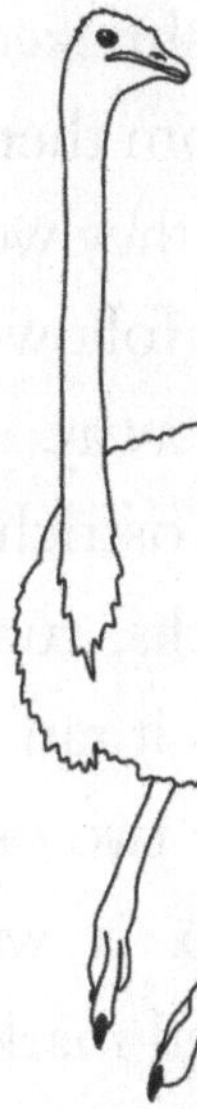

Chapter 17

As the sun rose the next morning, the children were unaware that the gate had opened, and that the farm worker had brought with him dozens of ostriches to graze in the field.

Rich woke with a loud cry. "What was that?" he shouted, rubbing his arm.

His shout woke Ems and Becks. They all jumped as they looked behind them to see a large beak and an enormous body. An ostrich had pecked Rich. Quickly moving before it had a chance to peck them again, they ran away. It was then they realised how many there were.

"Look at them all!" shrieked Ems. "How are we going to get away from them?"

Just as before when they were in the tractor, the ostriches started to follow alongside them, their beaks pecking away. They got the occasional nip from the ostriches as they ran.

"Aah!" shouted Becks, running quickly, an ostrich pecking at her as it ran along beside her. Ems was surrounded by two ostriches and Rich was getting nipped too. It wasn't particularly sore, but it did leave a red mark.

After a few minutes, the children realised that the ostriches weren't going to leave them alone, so they decided to jump over the fence to get away from them. Giving their arms and legs a rub where the ostriches had nipped them, they all agreed that they would wait a bit before going back in.

After about half an hour, the ostriches moved to the other end of the field. Feeling brave, the children climbed over the fence and started to look around the area just in front of it. They had ten minutes of searching before the ostriches realised that they were there and started to run over to them. Jumping back over the fence, they waited for another few minutes until they had gone again. For the next three hours this was repeated several times, the children looking at a small area and then running back over the fence when the ostriches saw them.

Feeling deflated, the children wondered what to do next.

"We've been looking for the rock for hours now. I'm beginning to wonder if it's here," said Ems.

"Me too," said Becks. "I hope we find it soon."

"Our things are still at the other end of the field, and I don't fancy a night in there with the ostriches pecking around," said Rich.

"We've checked out most of the field now and looked under all of the trees," said Becks. "The only place we haven't looked is on the more open ground, but there are certainly no obvious rocks just lying around the field."

"I wonder if one of us could go in while the other two keep the ostriches occupied over here," said Rich, an idea forming in his mind.

"Great idea," said Becks. "Since I'm the fastest I'll go in!"

"You don't need to rub it in," answered Ems and Rich, laughing.

The children ignored the ostriches at the fence, and they soon lost interest and wandered away. Becks took this opportunity to jump over and made her way to start searching in the left-hand corner. She had a few minutes of uninterrupted searching before the ostriches noticed her and started to come towards her. At that point, Ems and Rich started to bang on the fence, hoping that nobody else would hear them. Surprisingly, it worked quite well, and most of the ostriches came over to them.

A couple of the ostriches went over to Becks, but she just remained really still, and after pecking a few times, the birds lost interest and moved away. She continued to look again before the ostriches noticed her and came running over. Quickly she scrambled up a tree. She signalled to the others to wait a few minutes before starting to make the noise again to draw them away.

Becks made the signal and Rich and Ems started to hit the fence loudly. Eventually, the ostriches wandered over to the noise and Becks was able to resume her search. After a time scrabbling around in the soil she finally stood up and signalled to Rich and Ems. She had found the rock and was holding it up triumphantly. Quickly, she ran over to their belongings and gathered them in her arms. Sprinting to the gate, the ostriches soon saw her and started to run after her. Peck, peck, peck went their beaks at her arms and grasping at her hair. With one last spurt of energy, she jumped and glided gracefully over the gate.

Delighted to have Becks back, the children moved away from the gate. After having something to eat and drink, Rich consulted the map again to see where the next location was.

Rich looked a bit puzzled as he looked at the map. "It says we're to go to Gansbaai, but there's coordinates next to it and it looks as if the cross is in the ocean."

"How on earth are we going to get a rock from the ocean?" said Becks.

"I suppose we'll just have to see when we get there," he answered.

Going through the same routine as before, they twirled and whirled until they arrived in Gansbaai.

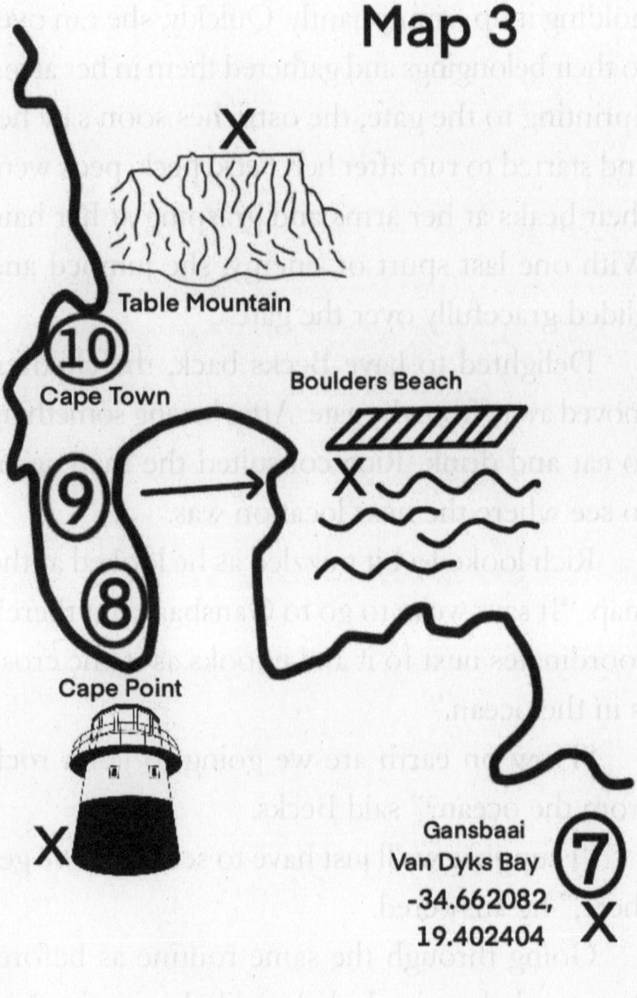
Map 3
Table Mountain
10
Cape Town
Boulders Beach
9
8
Cape Point
Gansbaai
Van Dyks Bay
-34.662082,
19.402404
7

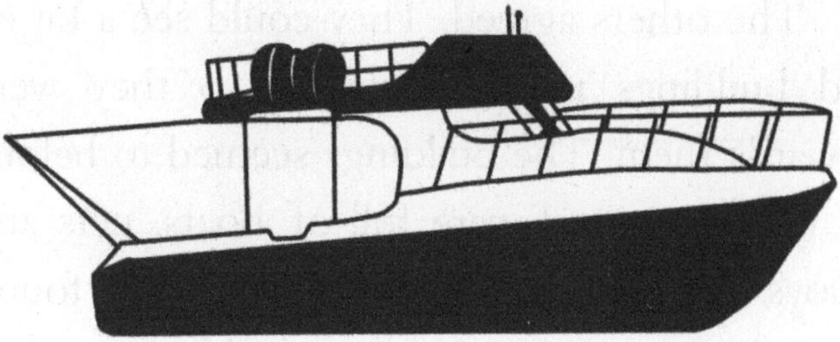

Chapter 18

Looking at the signs around them they realised that they were in shark territory. Gansbaai was renowned for being an excellent place to spot great white sharks.

Finding a spot on a huge boulder the children looked at the sea, mesmerised by the ebbing and flowing of the tide. They could see a lot of action further along the coast, with the boats filled with tourists returning.

Feeling a bit annoyed that they'd spent all day running away from the ostriches, they wondered what to do next.

"I think we're too late today to do anything," Becks said sensibly. "We can see what we can do tomorrow morning."

The others agreed. They could see a lot of old buildings in the distance, so they went towards them. The buildings seemed to belong to fishermen and were full of boats, nets and buoys. After trying several doors, they found one which was open and went inside.

An old boat was in the middle of the room, clearly being repaired and re-painted. The children climbed onto it and realised with delight that down the small steps there was a small bedroom. For the first time in several nights, they had somewhere comfortable to sleep. Within minutes they were snoozing, dreaming of being chased by ostriches, nightmares about being stalked by a lioness and being trapped in a mine.

As the sun rose early next morning, the children were awoken by the hustle and bustle of the fishermen getting ready for a day out at sea. Quickly, they got all their belongings together and crept out of the boat and the building that they had slept in.

Outside, fishermen were getting their nets ready, boats were being launched and tourists were starting to turn up to go on one of the tours. Double checking the map, Rich was still puzzled. "I still can't understand how the next rock can be in the ocean. There must be billions of rocks and stones on the ocean floor and anyway, it's so deep we would never get down there."

"I think we need to ask someone about the coordinates," said Ems, taking on the role as spokesperson again. She went over to two fishermen who were in the process of detangling nets and spoke to them.

A minute later, Ems waved enthusiastically for Rich and Becks to join her.

"Prince and Mosi here will take us out. I told them about our uncle who sadly died out there and they are happy to take us to the spot where his ashes were scattered," said Ems, nodding her head and winking furiously.

Rich was looking very confused, but Becks had cottoned on.

"That's amazing. Thank you so much for helping us. We couldn't afford to get a boat out.

As a thank you, we can help you with the nets, if you'd like. We have the coordinates of where our uncle lost his life," Becks said, giving them the details.

"We know exactly where that is," replied Mosi. "It's a dangerous area round here for sharks. You need to go out with a tour guide or someone who understands the ways of the ocean here."

"It's no bother to take you out," agreed Prince smiling. "It would be great if you could help with the nets though. Your fingers are a bit smaller, so it might be easier for you to untangle them."

"We also have a cage on the side of the boat if you fancy doing a shark cage dive. There are wetsuits on the boat I can lend you if you do," said Mosi.

"That would be amazing," replied Becks, her eyes shining at the prospect of this.

Prince showed them how to untangle the nets, and for the next hour they sat, working on the nets, and chatting with their two new friends. Prince and Mosi were both delighted to speak about their love of the ocean and of fishing. The hour passed quickly, and before they knew it, they were getting into the wetsuits and launching the boat onto the choppy ocean from Van Dyks Bay. It was quite a breezy day and, although they were enjoying the boat ride, before too long, they all started to feel a bit seasick. Breathing in deeply and trying to focus on the horizon didn't seem to help too much. Rich looked positively green and was now hanging with his face over the side of the boat.

Prince clambered down the boat towards them. He took one look at Rich and laughed.

"I take it you're not feeling too good, mate. Don't worry we aren't too far away from where you want to be. We're going to stop the boat in a minute, and you can do the shark cage dive."

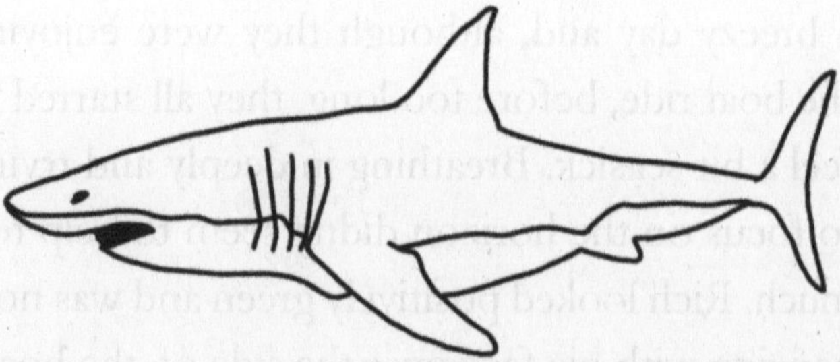

Chapter 19

Rich was looking more nervous now. Going into the water with predators didn't seem like his idea of fun. However, both Becks and Ems were buzzing with excitement as Mosi and Prince lowered the cage and made sure it was securely attached to the boat. Prince went to get some goggles for them, and Mosi started to throw chum into the sea. Mosi explained that the chum was to attract the sharks over. It was a mixture of tuna heads and fish guts.

Before long they could see a couple of fins coming towards the boat. It looked exactly like the fin that was in Jaws, the movie. In his mind, Rich could hear the theme tune, which made him feel even more nervous.

"Put your goggles on now and climb down the ladder into the cage," said Prince. "Don't put your fingers through the bars of the cage in case they get bitten!"

Rich looked even more worried now.

"You can hold onto the bars at the back of the cage or on the roof," continued Prince. "When I say 'down, down', take a deep breath and go under the water."

The children lowered themselves into the cage, and following Prince's instructions, they waited patiently. With their heads bobbing above the surface of the water they were able to see the shark fins in the distance.

"Down, down," shouted Prince.

The children all took a huge breath and went under the water. Looking through the goggles, they scanned the ocean in front of them. They could see a shape in the distance, but it didn't come any nearer. When they could hold their breath no more, they came up out of the water.

"That was a copper head shark," said Prince.

Mosi threw some more chum into the water, and they could see more sharks approaching. Bobbing about in the ocean with only a few metal bars to protect you from the sharks was quite unsettling, especially for Rich. He was out of his comfort zone doing this. Mosi attached a tuna head onto a large rod and put it in the water.

Before long, a shark caught the scent of it and came to the surface to grab it. From inside the cage, the children could see its pointed face and large, jagged teeth.

"Yes, that's a great white," Mosi confirmed. "Down, down."

Taking another deep breath, they went under again. This time they could see a shadow in the distance in the murky water, and it continued coming towards them. Within seconds, this huge creature with its pointed snout, huge teeth and large fins was within touching distance. Hearts pounding out of their chests, they watched as the great white changed direction at the last second to avoid colliding with the cage.

Gasping for breath as they came up, they could see the fin disappearing into the distance.

"Wow, that was amazing," Becks said with delight. "I thought it was going to hit the cage."

"I don't think I have been as nervous my whole life, apart from nearly being eaten by a lioness and being trapped down a mine," joked Rich, slowly recovering.

Mosi brought some blankets over for them, and a cup of tea from the thermos he had brought with him. They were all grateful for the help and care they were getting from Mosi and Prince.

Once the shark cage was back on board again, Mosi started up the boat and they made their way to the coordinates on the map. After about ten minutes, the boat stopped.

"Right, guys. This is the place you were looking for. There seems to be an old buoy here. It looks like it's been here for some time as it's pretty rusted and looks a bit deflated. We'll leave the three of you here and we'll go down below deck to give you some time," said Mosi kindly.

"Thank you. We appreciate that," said Becks.

The three children looked around them. Land was a long way in the distance. They could just make it out looking in one direction, and in the opposite direction was just an endless stretch of ocean with the horizon.

"There is nothing here except for that buoy. Do you reckon there is something there? If not, then I think we'll have failed in our quest, as we're never going to get down to the ocean floor. Even if we did, it would be like finding a needle in a haystack!" said Rich.

Becks and Ems made their way over so they could see the buoy, which was about five metres away. Looking from where they were, the children could see nothing obvious around it.

"I'll swim over to it," said Becks. "It's not far away. I'll be there and back before anything knows I'm in the water."

"I don't know about this," said Ems, looking nervous. "What if those sharks are still out there?"

"I agree with Ems. It's too risky to get into the water," Rich stated, nodding his head.

"There isn't really any alternative is there? It looks quiet for the moment," answered Becks, defiantly getting ready to go down the ladder.

The other two argued with her, but it was useless. She went into the water quietly so as not to alert the two men who were downstairs. Swimming the breaststroke, it only took her a few seconds to get over to the buoy. She quickly got to work looking all around it and then going under the water to see if there was anything there. After a few attempts she surfaced looking hopeful. Shouting over to Ems and Rich, she said that she could see something, but it needed untying.

With the shouts, the two men had come up and couldn't believe that Becks was in the water.

"What's happened?" shouted Mosi, alarmed by the situation. "Did she fall in?"

He quickly went to start the boat to take it nearer to the buoy. Meanwhile Prince had grabbed the life ring and was getting ready to throw it to her.

Rich had seen some activity in the water in the distance and realised that it was a group, or shiver, of sharks. "Quickly!" he shouted over to Becks.

"I can't get the knot undone," she shouted back desperately, going under the water again and again, undoing a small bit each time before she had to come up for a breath.

Prince had flung the life ring but was puzzled as to why Becks wasn't grabbing it. "Grab the ring and I'll pull you in!" he shouted to her.

By this time the boat was right next to the buoy and the sharks were getting nearer by the second. Whether they had noticed her in the water or were just passing made no difference, she had to get out - and quickly!

Becks suddenly came back up, triumphantly holding a rock, and quickly put the life ring over her. Prince pulled her in and dragged her up onto the boat.

"Are you okay?" said Mosi with concern. "What happened?"

The children all looked at each other, wondering what they could say. They knew they couldn't tell them the truth. Although they wanted to, they didn't know what the consequences would be.

Thinking quickly, Ems said, "We didn't want to say, but we knew that a family heirloom was attached to the buoy. We thought you wouldn't let us get it, but we know now we should have told you."

"If you had told us, we could have taken you closer for a look. Never mind – as long as you're safe, that's the main thing," said Prince.

Becks was wrapped in the blanket again and looking out of the boat at the shiver of sharks which had by now swum past the boat without giving it a glance. She was still smiling though, delighted that she had succeeded in her quest.

"Let's get you back to shore," said Mosi.

Half an hour later they were back in Gansbaai at the waterfront where they had started. Clambering out of the boat, the children all said thank you to Mosi and Prince. They were extremely grateful for all the two men had done for them and were sorry to leave them. Giving them a last wave, with the promise that they would keep in touch, the children got changed out of their wetsuits. The men said they could get a quick bite to eat at one of the tour buildings if they said they knew them. The children had a lovely lunch and chatted about their adventurous morning.

Becks brought out the rock she had found. From Rich's backpack, they took out the other rocks and started to lay them out on the table. They could see quite easily where the individual rocks went together. They now had two rows.

"Not too many to go," said Becks, looking overjoyed. "I just hope that the last few pieces of the puzzle are easier to find, with less drama."

"It really can't get much worse though, can it?" said Ems, smiling.

"Right, let's put these away and, fingers crossed, the next one will be easy and quick to find. Our parents will be wondering where we are. I feel terrible that we're letting them worry when we're actually okay, albeit in a strange kind of adventure," said Rich.

After consulting the map, the children moved to a quiet area outside the restaurant. They all touched the rock and shouted, "Cape Point."

Chapter 20

Landing with a roll and jumping straight into an upright position, Becks laughed as Rich still landed flat on the ground with a bump.

"One of these times I'll get it right," he laughed. "It's lucky we're all good at different things though. I don't think we would have got this far if we weren't."

"That's so true," said Ems, nodding her head in agreement. "With Becks and her sporting skills, you and your brain, and me with my love and knowledge of animals, we have worked really well together."

Looking at the landscape around them, they realised that they were still on the coast.

"We're at Cape Point. It looks like a lighthouse on the map," said Rich.

They were near the beach and walked over to the sign that said 'Cape of Good Hope. The most south-western point of the African continent.'

Pausing, they had a good look around. In the distance they could see a road, and walked to it. On their way, they could see baboons at the side. Very tame, they came over to the children to interact with them.

"Don't take any food out of the backpack whilst we're here, as that's what they're looking for," said Ems. "I know some people think it would be nice to feed the babies or young ones, but that's where the problem lies. The alpha male might see that as a threat and want either to challenge us, or they may take it out on the young."

"Wow!" said Becks. "I would never have known that. They look so cute too. I can see why people might think it's a good idea."

The children walked past them, not wanting to engage with them. It was lovely to see the family groups - the docile females enjoying the sun with their young close by, mothers feeding their babies, the larger ones playing and the alpha male keeping a close eye on things from afar.

Enjoying the walk in the sunshine, the children carried on along the path seeing many tourists in cars and buses arrive in the car park ahead of them. The lighthouse got nearer and nearer. They soon saw that they had to climb up a great number of steps to the lighthouse. There was also a funicular railway that took people up, but the children went to climb the steps. Becks managed this easily, but Ems and Rich definitely started to get slower the further up they got.

By the time they got to the top, they could see that the lighthouse was very old. An information plaque revealed that the lighthouse had been in use from 1860 to 1919 and could be seen by ships out at sea up to sixty-seven kilometres away. However, due to fog and cloud, it was often hidden due to its height above sea level. The Portuguese ship, the 'SS Lusitania', which was an ocean liner, was wrecked off Cape Point. Due to this, a new lighthouse was built that was a lot nearer to the sea level to prevent such tragedies from ever happening again.

There was also a signpost that showed how far Cape Point was from various cities in the world.

"Look, we're 9623 kilometres away from London," said Ems looking sad. "It feels like it's a long way away."

They all spent a few minutes just looking around at the view. Walking along a path, they could see the new lighthouse and it was certainly a lot lower than the original one was.

Rich brought out the map again and had a good look at it.

"It looks like the rock is quite near the old lighthouse. We can maybe have a quick look just now whilst there are people around, but if we can't find it, we may have to wait till the tourists are gone so we can have a better look and clamber on the rocks away from the paths."

"Yes, I think that's a good idea. We know what size the rocks are now, so it makes it slightly easier when looking," agreed Becks.

Making their way back to the old lighthouse, they started to study the rocks as they walked slowly past them. They got some funny looks from people as they did so, as it looked as though they had found something interesting as they were studying them so hard.

Laughing quietly to each other, the children continued to look. Becks was looking on one side of the path, and Rich and Ems on the other side. Before too long they were approaching the lighthouse again. Crowds had thinned down so they surmised that it couldn't be long until the park was closing.

"We need to find somewhere to shelter until everyone has gone home. We don't want to be found and escorted off," said Ems.

Quickly, they ran down the path, and when they couldn't see anyone, they carefully clambered over the rocks and through the bushes next to the path. They had to be cautious, as in parts the path had a sheer drop to the ocean.

At last, they found an overhanging rock that gave them the perfect shelter. Occasionally, they could still hear the odd voice as the last of the tourists left the area, and then after a while somebody whistling. Silently they sat for at least another hour just to be sure no one would be about.

"I don't hear anything now. I think it's probably safe enough to come out and go and look again," said Ems.

The other two nodded in agreement. Within minutes, they were back at the lighthouse. Looking around, they could see that there was a van still parked at the funicular station – the park ranger's. Keeping out of sight, the children started to explore properly, picking up any loose rocks and turning them over. They were so focused on searching for the rocks that they hadn't been aware of the impending fog coming towards them. It was only when Ems started to shiver that she looked up and saw that a dense fog was about to engulf them.

"Look at what's coming," she said to the others. Becks and Rich who were further away, looked up. Before they could move anywhere closer to each other, they were surrounded by it. This blanket of fog meant that they couldn't see more than about an arm's length in front of them.

"Just try and stay where you are until it passes," said Rich, sensibly. "If we start to move, we'll end up coming off the path and tumbling down into the ocean."

They all sat down where they were, rubbing themselves to keep warm as it was so cold and damp.

Chapter 21

Suddenly, a familiar rasping voice whispered from within the fog.

"You thought you could escape me. I clearly underestimated how good you are at swimming. I won't make that mistake again. But here you are. I can smell you. I can feel the fear going through you. There is nowhere for you to go."

The children all got to their feet and looked around, but there was absolutely nothing to be seen. Just grey, damp fog swirling in front of them. They could hear a swishing sound and then footsteps. Step. Step. Step. Then a pause.

It was difficult to know where the sound was coming from. The children were all quite disorientated and, having turned around, now had no idea which way they were facing. Holding out their hands and taking small cautious steps, they started to move, listening intently for any noise as they went.

Stopping every few seconds to listen. Becks was absolutely petrified. Not knowing which direction the hooded figure was coming from was a thing of nightmares. She knew she was on the path, but she wasn't sure which direction she was going in. Feeling along the path, she found the edge and quietly felt for the bushes and rocks at the side. She crawled on her hands and knees through it until she could feel a drop at the other side. With a start she realised that this was the drop down to the ocean. Pulling back half a metre or so, she curled into a ball and just waited and listened, shivering in the cold.

Meanwhile, Rich had started to crawl away, realising that he was on the path and as it sloped downwards, he knew he was heading away from the lighthouse. He still couldn't work out which direction the hooded figure was coming from though, so stopped to listen about every metre.

During this time, Ems, who was nearer to the lighthouse, realised that the rasping voice was coming from only a few metres away. She curled up at the side of the path, hoping that she wouldn't be found, trying hard to make no sound as the footsteps came nearer and nearer, closer, and closer.

Taking a deep breath, she held it as she felt the air change as the figure walked by just beside her. Ems could smell the stench coming from this ghastly figure and could feel the swish of the cloak as it walked past her. Just after it went by, it stopped and spoke again.

"I can smell your fear," it said, sniffing the air. "You would be better coming with me now, rather than waiting for the inevitable to happen."

The figure started to walk again slowly, taking each step one at a time. It passed by Becks, who was still hiding in the bushes at the side of the path. She felt her heart was beating really loudly and was worried that it would be heard. The figure passed on, obviously unable to see any better than the children. Rich, by this time, had been able to get most of the way down the path. As he got further down, the path widened and didn't have any steps for him to stumble over. As a result, he was able to move more quickly. It wasn't long before he found himself at the funicular station. He quickly went inside and hid in a corner.

The hooded figure stopped and turned around, having heard a noise behind it. There were some baboons, who were also finding it difficult to see in the thick fog.

"Go away!" the hooded figure shouted at them. However, to the young baboons, the large cloak that it was wearing seemed the ideal place to shelter in. Before long, there were several baboons all trying to immerse themselves under the cloak into a sheltered space.

All Ems and Becks could hear were the grunts, barks and wahoos of the baboons. The barks were to ensure that any other baboons who were lost in the fog would be able to find them. It was evident from the noises that the figure had many baboons around it and was struggling to get them away.

"Leave me alone!" it shouted, swishing the cloak away from them and trying to move away unsuccessfully. Eventually, it gave a long, anguished scream.

"Don't be thinking you're safe - I still have time to find you before the end of the quest. I'm determined to do my bit to stop Michael. He was going to get rid of us all with his magic. Michael said magic should only be used for good. Rubbish! Magic can be used for whatever you want."

With that, there was an almighty crack and then silence, apart from the confused baboons who had lost their shelter.

Ems and Becks, who had heard all this, gave a sigh of relief. Rich was still none the wiser in the building at the bottom of the hill. The fog by this time had started to shift slowly and within five minutes, there was more visibility. Becks started to crawl out of the place she had been hiding and back to the path, and Ems stood up looking around trying to see the others. Ems and Becks soon found each other and with the fog clearing all the time, it wasn't long before Rich came out of the building. He peered around the side of it, as he hadn't seen or heard what had happened up nearer the lighthouse. Ems and Becks soon spotted him and ran down the path to see him. They quickly filled him in with the details of what had happened.

"That was lucky the baboons came along just at the right time," said Rich.

"Yes, if the figure had walked past me again I'm sure it would have seen me, especially as the fog had started to lift. I would have been in plain view," said Ems, remembering with a shiver.

Becks agreed and also mentioned that she'd had a close call with the edge of the cliff. "It was lucky that I was going so slowly, or else I would have fallen into the ocean."

Relieved that they were all okay and had managed to survive another encounter with the mysterious hooded figure, they went back up the hill to resume their search for the rock. Starting from where they had left earlier, they managed a few more minutes of searching before realising that time was limited, as it was about to get dark. They made their way down to where Rich had been hiding and settled there for a few hours.

As the sun rose, so did the children, keen to get started on the searching before the tourists arrived. Starting from the lighthouse, they decided to stray away a bit from the path now. The children all looked in the bushes at the side of the path, and around the larger rocks that were there. After a couple of hours of looking and just before the gates to the park opened for tourists, they struck gold (or rather rock!).

"Thank goodness," said Ems, relieved that she had found it. The rock had been wedged between another two larger ones and had been hidden by a bush. She handed it to Rich and just as she did so, a rather large male baboon came up and grabbed it out of Rich's hand.

"Oi!" shouted Rich, as it scampered away, making noises to the other baboons as it went.

The children all took to their heels and started to run after it, shouting as they ran. The other baboons all started to grunt and bark as they tried to keep up with their family member. Slowing down to a walk, they saw that the baboon had stopped on some rough ground away from the path and was examining the rock.

"I wonder if it thought it was food. I can't imagine that it really wants a rock," said Ems. "Maybe get that last cake out of the bag, and let's see if we can swap it."

All the baboons were now together, making lots of excited noises. The children approached them cautiously watching the baboons constantly. The baboons watched back, probably wondering what the children were doing.

Rich went forward slowly and put the food on the ground near them. The baboons, realising what it was, went wild and all started to make their way over to it. The male baboon took one last look at the rock and then decided to throw it at the children.

Becks took a leap into the air and managed to catch it with both hands.

"Let's get away from the baboons while they're occupied," she said. "I don't know what would have happened if the rock had smashed when they threw it. Would we still be able to use it?"

"I don't know, and I don't want to find out," said Ems.

Rich took the map out and had a look at it. "We have to go to Boulders Beach next."

All putting their fingers on the rock, they shouted, "Boulders Beach," and they soon found themselves landing there.

Chapter 22

"I have no idea what Boulders Beach is," said Rich, looking a bit confused as he looked around. "I'm hoping it's not a huge beach with miles of sand for us to search through."

As they walked along the boardwalk, seeing some dassies on the way, they soon noticed that there were other creatures there – penguins. Reading some of the signs, the children were interested to learn that they were African Penguins and were an endangered species. The colony around Boulders Beach was set up to protect the penguins from the increasing threat of marine pollution, global warming, overfishing, problems with pets, tourism activities and destruction of their habitat.

The penguins build their nests in the sand or sometimes under rocks or bushes. They have a black stripe and have a pattern of black spots on their chests. There were a few of them next to the boardwalk, and some were making their nests and others just sitting on them.

Ems, Rich and Becks took their time just watching these delightful creatures, being aware all the time that although they might look cute, they shouldn't put their fingers anywhere near them if they didn't want a nip.

"After being in the ostrich farm, I think I've had quite enough of birds and their beaks," said Ems laughing. The other two agreed and ensured that their fingers were well away from them.

Before too long they had reached the final boardwalk where they could go through the visitor centre and out to see most of the penguins on Foxy Beach. Noticing that they would have to pay to get in, they quietly crept through an open side door.

They walked along the boardwalk next to the beach and saw hundreds of penguins. Some were in the water, swimming and diving, others were happy grooming and preening themselves or their mate, and some were in their nests. No matter where the children looked, they were surrounded by penguins. Seeing them in their natural habitat was amazing and knowing that they were not disturbing their breeding ground by being on the boardwalk added to the experience.

"There is just so many of them," Ems said gleefully. "Look at the chicks too, interacting with the mother."

They stood for a long time watching the penguins moving along the boardwalk, so they didn't miss a single view of them. The penguins were quite comical, waddling about, digging in the sand to make their nests and making a loud donkey-like sound.

Eventually, they had to get back to the reality of finding the rock. Bringing out the map again, Rich saw that the rock was in the area around the boardwalk where the penguins were.

"It's here somewhere," he said, looking out at the beach around him. "I'm not sure how we'll find it though. There's a lot of sand and penguins.

Surely a rock could have been swept out to sea or been taken away by developers."

"I was wondering that too - maybe there is some magic attached to the rocks so that they remain in place. Let's just hope this isn't any different," answered Ems.

"We're going to need to come back later when no one else is here. There are lots of rocks over there so that would be the obvious place to start looking, plus it looks like we could investigate there without disturbing the penguins too much," said Becks.

The children left the beach and started to walk back to where they had first landed. Sitting on the rocks there, they emptied the rucksack to see what they had left. A couple of packets of crisps, a packet of biscuits and some small oranges was all that remained. Rich remembered seeing a water fountain at the visitor centre, so he went back along to refill the water bottles.

Sitting there they finally had a chance to relax for a few hours, enjoy the view and doze in the sun.

Shortly after the visitor centre closed, and everything had quietened down, the children felt they could nip over the fence and over to the larger rocks at the far end of the beach without being noticed. Careful not to disturb the penguins that were nesting just off the boardwalk, the children stepped carefully through the maze of nests.

Arriving at the rocks within a few minutes, they started to look. With dusk not too far away, the children split up and searched a different area each.

They were lucky, within about ten minutes of searching, Rich suddenly shouted the girls over.

"I think that's it there," he said, pointing in between two larger rocks. "I think I can see the map drawings on it."

Sure enough when the girls looked at it, they both agreed. Using all their strength they managed to move one of the large rocks, which was enough to allow them to get the smaller rock out.

Rich looked at it but made a grunt at the same time. Turning it over, he examined it more closely.

"What's up? Is it the wrong rock?" asked Becks.

"No, it's the right rock but it appears to be broken. Part of the map isn't there," he said, looking crestfallen. "There must be about five square centimetres missing. Hopefully it will be okay."

The girls had a look at it too and agreed with Rich that part of the rock was definitely missing.

"All we can do is try using it and hope for the best," said Becks, trying to look optimistic.

They all placed their finger on it and said, "Table Mountain," which was the last place on the map they were to visit.

Expecting to move straight away, they braced themselves for the twirling and swirling - but it never came. Rich had been determined that he was going to land a bit more gracefully for one of his last attempts, so he was disappointed when it didn't happen.

"Well, that didn't work, did it?" said Ems, shrugging her shoulders.

"Let's try it again. Maybe one of us didn't have our finger on it!" wondered Becks, thinking positively.

They tried it again and again, each time adapting something - shouting, putting their whole hand on it - until they could think of nothing else to do.

"Looks like we're stuck here," said Rich, looking dejected.

"Why don't we wait till the morning and try again? It's getting late now," Ems said sensibly, but looking rather worried.

"What happens if we can't get it to work?" Becks said, becoming upset. "What if we've come all this way and can't finish the jigsaw?"

"I think we'll be okay. It just means we'll have rather a long walk to get to Table Mountain," Ems replied, trying to cheer the other two up.

"Aah, so we will," agreed Rich. "I hadn't thought of that. Of course, we can just walk there. Why don't we get some sleep and wake up when the sun rises? We can try again, and if it doesn't work, we can start to walk?"

"That sounds like a plan," answered Becks, sounding a bit more cheerful.

They moved to a sheltered spot just beyond the rocks that had bushes round it. The children found it difficult to get to sleep, probably because this day had been less exhausting than the other days they'd had recently. Sleeping in fits and starts throughout the night, they struggled to get comfortable, but were soothed by the gentle sound of the waves ebbing and flowing. By the time sunrise came, they were wide awake and watched the beautiful sight of the sun appearing in the horizon and the sky becoming brighter.

Rich got the rock out and they tried to use it as a portal a few more times. However, it was hopeless, so they gathered their belongings and started to walk out to the main road.

Chapter 23

Managing to locate a road sign within the first few minutes, they were reassured they were going in the right direction. It read 'Cape Town - 40 kilometres.'

"How long will that take us?" asked Ems, looking at Rich.

Rich quickly did some calculations in his head.

"Roughly eight hours, give or take," he replied. "If we start walking now, we'll hopefully get there by the end of the day, and we can think about climbing Table Mountain tomorrow."

The hours passed fairly quickly as they walked in the sun. It was lovely to walk along next to the beach passing through Fish Hoek, then cutting inland for a while and back to the beach at Hout Bay. Before they knew it, nearly six hours had passed without a complaint from any of them. As they approached the outskirts of Cape Town, they found themselves feeling quite weary and hungry. Knowing they had completed three quarters of the walk already, they all felt pleased with themselves. They were so busy feeling proud that they hadn't realised that they had gone off course. Starting to feel a bit self-conscious, they looked around as they felt they were being watched. Inadvertently, they had walked into one of the townships that surrounded Cape Town.

Rich knew immediately where they were.

"I think we've walked into one of the townships."

Ems wasn't sure she understood what he meant.

Rich continued, "They are underdeveloped built up areas on the outskirts of cities where black Africans were forced to live during apartheid. Some of them still live there even although apartheid is abolished."

Looking around, the children could see poverty on a scale they could only have imagined. Shipping containers were split into two to accommodate two families, makeshift huts built using wood and corrugated iron, and some buildings used to house lots of families. As they were looking, a group of young children came out to play just in front of them - happy and laughing, playing with a ball. Their infectious laughter made Ems, Rich and Becks laugh, and before they knew it, they were playing a game of football with them. Becks was keen to show off her football skills and the boys from the township were impressed.

Before too long, they were talking about football, especially about some of the Premier League teams which the children in the township were very enthusiastic about. One of the older boys, whose name was Kofi, was very friendly and was interested to know why they were there.

Becks answered that they were on their way to Table Mountain but had got a bit lost.

Kofi invited them to have something to eat with his family. The children looked at each other knowing that his family would have probably worked hard to get enough money to put a meal on the table, but also knew that these were proud people, and they would do anything to help someone in need.

Ems answered, "We would love to eat with you. Thanks for asking."

Kofi took them through the narrow streets, chattering on the way and explaining what they were seeing as they went.

Many of the families had been there since the times of apartheid when black people had to live in separate areas to white people. Many of them have had to stay, as the prices are just too high for them to move anywhere else but they have also built up a wonderful community there. Although times were hard, the families all helped each other out. Kofi took them into a church, and they were able to hear the uplifting songs and messages that were being given. They walked past some stalls which were selling sheep's heads, locally produced beer and other local delicacies.

Stopping at a large open area, they could see some women cooking and lots of people around.

Kofi introduced them to his family, who were all delighted to see them, especially the young children who loved having someone to play with. The food smelt delicious and before long they were tucking into traditional South African food.

Sitting on the ground eating boerewors (sausage) and Kota (bread hollowed out with a filling), they thought it was delicious. Afterwards, they played with the young children and before long it started to get dark. Kofi said he could give them something to sleep on outside and the children accepted this gratefully. Kofi said his father knew someone with a minibus who would take them round Cape Town and up to the base of Table Mountain in the morning.

The next day, they were awoken by the early morning hustle and bustle of people going to work and school and cooking breakfast outdoors. By eight o'clock, they had waved goodbye to Kofi and his family, with promises of keeping in touch. They were relieved to be going in the minibus for the next part of their journey, as they were anticipating the hike up Table Mountain would be a huge challenge.

John, the driver, took them in the minibus on a tour of Cape Town, showing them the Olympic

Stadium, the Royal Residence, the statue of Nelson Mandela outside the Town Hall and then St George's Cathedral. They also saw the benches that were marked 'Whites Only' and 'Non-Whites Only' outside the magistrate's court as a reminder of apartheid. They passed by the Victoria and Albert Waterfront, which is popular for shopping, restaurants and entertainment.

After the tour, the minibus took them past Camps Bay and Sea Point round to the road leading up to Table Mountain. John told them that Table Mountain is 1086 metres or 3563 feet above sea level. It seemed a long way up!

They were dropped off at the foot of Platteklip Gorge and after saying thank you and goodbye, looked up at the awe-inspiring Table Mountain towering above them. It was amazingly flat at the top and looked really high. Already they could see groups of people making their ascent up the mountain, trudging up the steep zig zagging path to the top.

"Right, we have got plenty of water and some food to keep us going. It should take us a few hours to get to the top. Hopefully, we'll find this last stone quickly and can get home today," said Ems, feeling positive.

Rich was looking a bit worried. "I hope I won't keep you back. I don't think I'll be very fast going up. I'm exhausted already just looking at it. My leg is still hurting too."

"It'll be fine," said Becks encouragingly. "We'll all go up together. If we need to stop a lot, that's okay. As long as we all reach the top with each other."

They started to walk along the path which got steadily steeper as they walked. The views overlooking Cape Town were fantastic. Catching a glimpse of some of the wildlife within Table Mountain National Park, such as various types of antelope like the springbok and steenbok, polecats and mongooses, made the walk extra special. Taking regular rests as they ascended the gorge, the path weaved back and forth and, as they climbed higher, the rocky steps got steeper. Sometimes, they had to give each other a hand to climb up some of the larger steps.

"We're getting there," smiled Becks to the others. Ems nodded in agreement. Rich, however, was struggling a bit and they were having to take regular rests now. It meant that they could admire the views around them. The girls both stopped at different times too, so it wasn't always Rich who was asking to stop. They were trying hard to be encouraging and to not let him feel deflated.

Nearing the top with every step, they soon found themselves at the bottom of a roped section. This was very steep and required the use of the handrail to pull themselves up the final part. At last, after about three hours of climbing, they had reached the summit. Walking along the flat top, they made their way to the lookout sections.

From the top, the views were amazing. They could see another hill - the Lions Head - as well as the Olympic stadium, Robben Island and the Victoria and Albert Waterfront. It was such a clear day that they could make out the boats out at sea and some cars on the roads. Moving round to the other side, they were able to see Camps Bay, where they had just driven from that morning.

"What an achievement!" Rich said, looking tired but very pleased with himself. "I must admit there were times when I thought that I couldn't go on anymore. Thanks though. If it hadn't been for you two encouraging me, I don't think I would have made it."

"No worries. It was a tough climb, but I'm glad we did it rather than use the cable car. No one will believe us when we go home and tell them about our adventures," Becks said happily.

"People will think we're crazy," said Ems, with a smile. "We will have to tell them something though. Where is the last rock, I wonder?"

Rich brought out the map and they studied it hopefully, for the last time.

"It looks like it's somewhere over there," Rich said, pointing. "There are lots of rocks up here though so we may take a while to find it."

There were quite a few tourists at the top taking photographs, selfies and eating. Walking around the paths, they saw that many of the rocks were actually too big, and that the number of smaller ones was minimal. Each taking a different area, they split up and started to look. Searching around, they began picking up different rocks and scrutinising them carefully to see if there were any markings on them. After a short while, they came together to discuss where to tackle next, then off they went again.

There were fewer people coming up the gorge now, as for them to get back down the same way would take the remaining time before it got dark. People were still coming up in the cable car and walking around the summit. There was some heat in the air, despite them being at the top of the mountain.

Suddenly, there was a sharp change in temperature. Extra jumpers were brought out the bag and put on. Looking around, the children didn't see any clouds. The sun was still out and reasonably high in the sky.

Out of nowhere, from behind a large rock appeared the hooded figure.

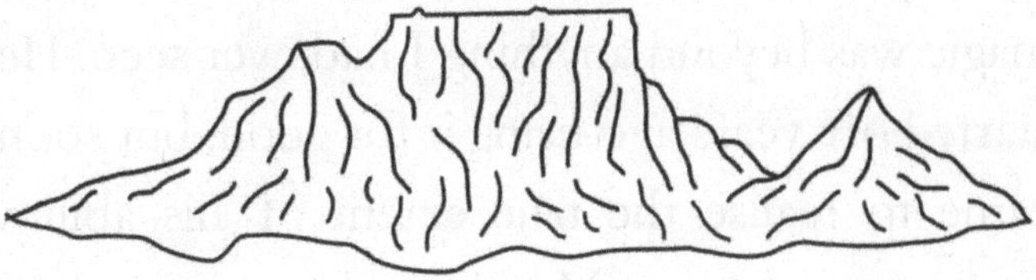

Chapter 24

Becks literally fell to the floor, shaking uncontrollably.

Ems stood up tall and Rich put the backpack on his back properly.

"What do you want?" asked Ems, looking braver than she felt.

In the quiet rasping voice, the hooded figure spoke, "Well, here we are again. I didn't expect you to still be here. You do know I can't let you go home. I'm one of the guardians of magic, and I have to do the job I agreed to all those years ago, and not let Michael come back again."

Rich tentatively asked, "Why? What did Michael do that was so bad?"

The voice responded, "Michael was the most powerful magician there ever was. His magic was beyond anything I had ever seen. He started off years ago using it for good, but soon came to realise the true extent of his ability. Unfortunately, our Magic Circle was too late. Michael had become a Master of Magic and had started to create havoc across the world - mysterious fires, droughts, governments falling apart. We tried to shut him down, but he was just too powerful. Eventually, we all got together with a plan to prevent further destruction around the world. It would cost us though. Michael knew we were trying to stop him, so in his garden he left clues in the form of rocks and the jigsaw in the attic, hoping that one day someone would come along to complete it and let him back out in the world to finish off what he had started. We all assembled at his house, but before we could do anything he had put a curse on us. All of us left writhing about in many horrific forms – this is what he did to me!" pointing at itself.

"Why should we believe you? You have only wanted to hurt us since we got here and prevent us from getting back home. We want to see our families again. The statue is of a young boy who can't be older than about sixteen. There is no way he could have done what you say. We would have heard about it from somewhere," Ems said bravely.

"After cursing us all, we managed to summon enough magic to turn him into a statue, with each magician putting a spell on a different part of the body. When each part of the puzzle is solved, the spell is lifted and that part of him will no longer be stone. I'm sorry, but I just can't risk you getting home and lifting part of the spell." As it spoke, from underneath its cloak, its true self was revealed.

Clothes as dark as the midnight sky, a stench worse than anything you had ever smelt before and the face, well, if you could call it a face, was only partially there. Half skeletal, half rotting, it was the stuff of nightmares.

The children gasped and started to back away, falling over the stones as they went. Within seconds, the figure started to chant a spell. Pebbles, stones, rocks and boulders all started to lift off the ground. The children looked round amazed as the rocks hovered in the air.

Ems soon realised what was about to happen.

"Find somewhere to hide, cover your head!" she shouted.

Rich and Becks started to run with their hands over their heads to protect them.

Almost immediately, the stones, pebbles and rocks started to move around them. Crash, bang, they went. Becks had managed to run quite far before they started moving, although was still getting hit by them. Rich hid behind a huge boulder which at that moment had not moved. Despite being shielded by the boulder, he was still getting hammered by rocks and stones from all directions.

Ems had managed to find some shelter too, although the rocks and stones seemed to locate her.

All three peering through their fingers managed to avoid some of the bigger rocks that were moving around. By now, they'd been hit numerous times over their bodies, and were definitely going to have lots of bruises.

What they did notice was that the other tourists who were standing a bit away from them seemed oblivious to what was going on.

Within two or three minutes, the stones and rocks suddenly all dropped out of the air to the ground. Feeling relieved, the children looked around trying to spot the hooded figure. It was still there and looked like it was chanting something else.

The next minute, just above the children, enormous clouds suddenly appeared in the sky. Torrential rain started to pour down, and gusty winds rampaged over the top of Table Mountain.

Visibility became very hard. Soaked through and nearly getting blown away from the position that they were crouched in, the children managed to remain where they were.

"Look over here," the rasping voice said through the noise of the rain and wind.

Their hands over their eyes, the children managed to look through the heavy rain.

"I have found it," the figure said, holding onto the last rock.

The children's hearts all sank as they realised the hopelessness of the situation they were in.

"You'll never get home now. The only way is through the portal. Tell anyone about this and you die."

Racking their brains, the children tried to think of a way out of this. Before any of them could speak, Ems had risen from the spot where she was crouched and was running straight for the hooded figure. She was coming from the side. The hooded figure hadn't seen her as it was too busy looking at the rock. It didn't hear Ems approach because of the loud wind and rain. Just feet away from it, Ems launched herself off the ground, landing squarely on the figure, moving it back a few feet. Then they disappeared!

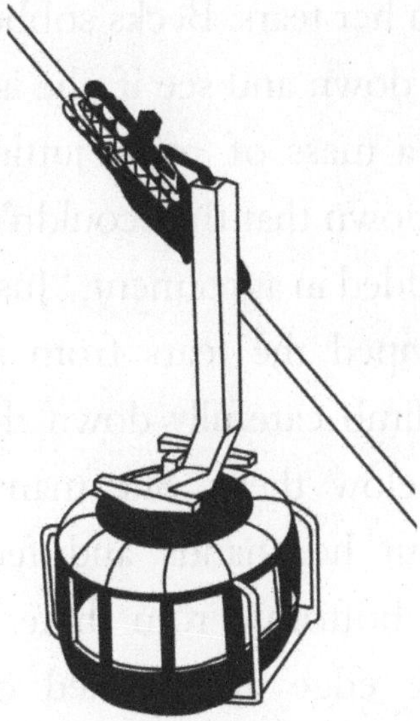

Chapter 25

Rich and Becks both screamed at the same time and rushed to where they had vanished over the side of Table Mountain. It was only while they were running that they realised that the rain and wind had ceased. As they got closer to the edge, they got to their hands and knees and started to crawl over, not wanting to risk the same fate. Peering over the edge, their eyes darted back and forth desperate to see some movement from below.

Becks by this point was crying and screaming for Ems. Rich was looking distraught.

Through her tears, Becks sobbed, "I think I could climb down and see if she is over there," pointing to a mass of rocks jutting out about two metres down that they couldn't see beyond.

Rich nodded in agreement, "Just be careful."

Becks wiped the tears from her face and started to climb carefully down the two-metre rock face below them. She managed to find places to put her hands and feet and soon reached the bottom. From there, she gingerly went to the edge and looked over. To her delight, there was Ems just below, clinging on for dear life on a small ledge.

"Ems!" Becks shouted above her.

Ems looked up nervously and broke into a smile when she saw Becks. She was standing on a ledge about a metre long, but only about a quarter of a metre wide. Below that there was a steep, rocky cliff face. If she had tumbled over that, there was no way she would have survived.

Becks could see that there weren't really any places for her feet and hands to go, and that she wouldn't be strong enough to hoist her back up. Besides, if anything went wrong, she would hurtle to her death. Making a quick assessment, she saw that it would be dangerous for them to try and help without proper equipment. She said this to Ems, who agreed. Ems was petrified to move even a little bit and after looking below her, she felt sick with terror. Concentrating now on the horizon in front of her was preferable to looking down.

Becks shouted to Rich to go and get help, as there was nothing they could do to help Ems without putting her in even more danger. He agreed and ran off to raise the alarm.

Becks tried to reassure Ems, who was looking paler by the minute. She asked Ems what had happened with the hooded figure. Just as she was about to respond, they could hear movement from above. Help had arrived!

Two professional climbers who had just reached the top, coming up one of the other steep paths, had said that they could help if she wasn't injured. Using the climbing ropes and harnesses, they soon attached them to an anchor at the top where Rich was.

Within minutes, one of the climbers, Cathy, was making her way down to Ems. Once there, she got Ems very carefully, into the harness.

Lifting each foot slowly and then moving the harness up under her thighs and attaching it to the carabiner and belay, she was soon ready to go. With Cathy giving her reassurance and pointing out where to put her feet, Ems slowly made her way up the rock face, with the other climber, Joe, assisting in controlling the rope. He would be able to stop Ems from falling if she were to slip. Regardless of her fear, Ems made it to where Becks was, and then with minimal help climbed to where Joe and Rich were. Cathy and Becks came up after Ems, and they had an emotional reunion at the top.

"What happened?" asked Cathy.

Not wanting to give anything away, Ems replied, "I was just looking over the edge and a gust of wind came. I lost my balance and fell over the side."

"You were lucky to land where you did. Another centimetre and you'd have fallen down that steep ravine," Cathy replied. "It was fortunate we were here with all the correct equipment, as it's starting to get dark now."

"We are very grateful for your help. Thank you so much," Ems replied, on behalf of the other two as well.

Escorting them to the cable car, Joe and Cathy paid for them to go down with them.

"This is so kind of you," said Becks. "We wouldn't have liked to have walked all the way back down again."

"I'm not lying, I'm not sure I would've managed that. I was exhausted coming up," said Rich honestly.

Looking out over Cape Town, they could see the sun starting to set. It looked beautiful in the disappearing light. When they got to the bottom, they thanked Cathy and Joe again and made their way as if they were waiting for someone to pick them up. Giving them a last wave, they disappeared behind a large van. They waited there until they could see the car that Joe and Cathy were in disappear.

"Thank goodness, you're okay," said Becks again. "What on earth made you run at that awful creature?"

"I couldn't think of what else we could do. It was a spur of the moment decision," replied Ems.

"Well, I wonder what happened to the hooded figure and our rock. I don't think we are ever going to find it now," said Rich, looking dismayed.

"When I landed on the hooded figure, we ended up moving backwards until we fell off the top, and landed where you were, Becks. We fought a bit and then fell off the ledge. I managed to grab onto the rock face, but the figure went right over. I had a quick look below once I had got myself stable, but I couldn't see anything," said Ems.

"What do we do now?" asked Rich, looking downtrodden.

"I do have something though to cheer you up. When I was wrestling with the hooded figure, I managed to get the rock from its grasp!" Ems said with excitement, brandishing the elusive rock. The final piece of the jigsaw!

Becks squealed with delight. Rich punched the air. They all hugged each other. The last rock to complete the jigsaw map.

Going over to the side, Rich emptied the other nine rocks from his backpack. Looking at all the rocks together they could see a pattern emerging. Moving them piece by piece, they soon had them in a three-by-three formation.

Faint lines could be seen joining each rock to the next. A map very much like the one they had been using was now in front of them. They could see all the areas where they had visited; Blyde River Canyon, the goldmine, Kruger National Park, Addo Elephant National Park, Storms River Mouth, the ostrich farm, shark territory, Cape Point, and the broken rock that was Boulders Beach.

"Where do you think the Table Mountain rock goes?" asked Becks, looking confused.

"Its markings are different to all the others," Rich agreed, looking equally as perplexed.

It appeared to have some words on it rather than part of a map. Looking closely, they could just about make out what it said.

"It looks like it says "Tuiste," said Becks. "Well, why don't we put the rock on top of the middle of the square and put our finger on it and say the word. We may as well give it a try."

All three of them were feeling excited about the prospect of going home, but also nervous at what they would find when they returned.

Putting one arm around each other, they all put their fingers on the stone and said the magic word. Nothing happened. They tried again - still nothing.

"I hope it's not because of the broken rock," said Rich. "Let's try to pronounce it differently this time and see if that makes a difference."

After trying a few times, they began to despair. On a whim, Becks took the rock and ran over to a bus driver who was just about to leave with a coach full of tourists.

"Excuse me, can you tell me what this says please?" she asked politely.

The young man looked at it and said, "Tuiste. It means home." He repeated it another couple of times, with Becks echoing it after him.

"Thank you," she said, running back to the others.

She repeated what he had said, and the others noted it was quite different to the way they had been pronouncing it.

Trying again, they shouted the name together, their fingers on the rock.

Whoosh! They hurtled into oblivion, spinning and turning as before. Seconds later they were flung out again, their best landing yet (they'd had a lot of practice!).

Looking around they saw to their amazement that they were back in the attic room, with the jigsaw in front of them, completely intact.

Chapter 26

Pinching each other to make sure they were really there, they hugged and screamed with glee.

"I can't believe it worked!" shrieked Ems, overjoyed.

Tears of joy were streaming down Becks' face. Rich looked so happy.

"Let's go and see what's been happening. I hope we're not in too much trouble," he said.

Running down the stairs, Ems shouted "Mum, Dad! We're back!"

"Back from where?" joked Dad. "Did you get lost up in the attic? What's up there anyway?"

The three children looked at each other.

"How long have we been up there for?" asked Ems looking puzzled.

"I don't know, a couple of hours maybe," Dad answered, looking at them all closely. "You've got bruises all up your arms and your clothes are filthy. Is it that bad up there?"

"Yes, it's really dirty, and there's lots of stuff to move about," they all agreed, nodding.

"Go and grab a snack, whilst we finish off in here," Dad said as he walked away.

The three children went into the kitchen and made themselves a sandwich. They had forgotten how hungry they were with all the drama on top of Table Mountain.

Sitting stuffing their faces at the table, they recalled all their adventures.

"I can't believe that no time has passed," said Rich. "We were there for days! I'm just glad that the broken rock made no difference to the final jigsaw. I thought it might not have worked like it did when we used it on its own."

"I'm so glad our families didn't realise we had gone. What happens now with the jigsaw?" said Becks. "Is that it all over now?"

"I'm not sure. I hope so," said Ems.

The three children got up and headed outside. Looking around the garden, they sensed a change.

"Something's different," said Ems, looking puzzled.

Walking around the garden, they got an uneasy feeling that they were being watched.

"Come over here!" shouted Rich.

The girls ran over to where he was standing in front of the statue.

"Does something look strange to you?"

"I'm not sure," Ems said, looking at the statue.

"It's the leg," cried Becks. "It's changed colour. It looks kind of new, rather than old and crumbling like the rest of it."

"That's odd," Ems said. "I didn't say before, but when I got up to go to the toilet the night before our adventure, I thought that the statue had moved. I was looking out from the hall window. I just assumed it was my imagination, especially since I'd just woken up."

They looked closely at the statue, and then remembered the rocks that were in the garden.

Becks slowly realised something.

"Does this mean that the rocks in the garden with the strange markings match the ones on our map?"

"Yes," said Rich. "Let's see if we can find them."

They split up and hunted for the rocks which they had found previously. Ems found the one they were looking for.

"It's exactly the same as the South Africa map we put together with all the rocks. The only difference is that you can hardly make out the markings on it."

"Do you reckon this means that there are other puzzles to do? Other countries to visit?" questioned Becks.

"Yes, it looks like it. The hooded figure was trying to kill us all the time we were in South Africa because it said that if we succeeded in completing the jigsaw, a powerful magician would be released. It said that there would be other monsters released too," Rich answered.

"Well, we managed to defeat the first one. I think we need to try and help poor Michael, if he's been imprisoned here all this time," said Becks.

"He looks like a normal boy, just a bit older than us, certainly. I think we should try and help him as I don't believe what the hooded figure told us. The magicians or monsters all come back to life one at a time when we complete the jigsaw, so they don't want us to find all the pieces as they don't want to disappear forever. It has nothing to do with Michael coming alive again. I wonder if we manage to complete all the jigsaws, he will gradually come to life," Ems said enthusiastically.

"We need to try and help him - although I would like a few days to recover after all our adventures," Becks said.

"That's settled then. In a few days let's complete the jigsaw again and see where we go to," Rich said.

"Let's call this The Jigsaw Mysteries," Ems said, smiling and putting her arms around the other two.

"Until the next time!"

Coming Soon!

Further books in The Jigsaw Mysteries.

Where will Ems, Rich and Becks go to next to solve the mystery?

About the Author

Elaine lives in the small village of Eaglesham in the Southside of Glasgow with her husband Craig, and their three children, Emily, Christopher and Rebecca.

She loves spending time with her family and friends, reading, completing jigsaws and going for long walks. While doing the jigsaws she came up with the idea of using them as a basis for her stories about a trio of children who travel to different countries to solve mysteries.

Elaine wrote her first book on South Africa after a fantastic holiday there. She used the places she travelled to within South Africa as the foundation for the adventures for Ems, Rich and Becks.

She loves nothing more than planning itineraries for holidays and visiting new and exciting places. Elaine loves to experience and see the tourist hotspots, go on beautiful walks and immerse herself in the culture and vibrancy of different areas in Scotland, the United Kingdom and the wider world.

Acknowledgements

Writing this book wouldn't have been possible without a few people.

Thank you to Michael Heppell and the 'Write That Book' Masterclass. I wouldn't have known where to start without you.

I'm grateful to the lovely folk I have met from the 'Write That Book' Scottish Meet-ups for answering all my questions about the publishing process and for being so welcoming.

I would like to give special thanks to my 'Emerging Butterflies' group for keeping me going and for encouraging me to 'Write That Book'. Thank you to Charmaine, Debra, Erika, Jane, Judith, Lis, Mark, Penny and Sam.

Thanks to my Book Group ladies who have opened my mind to other genres of books and have been interested in my writing.

A huge thank you to my dad, Ronnie, and all my other family and friends who have encouraged me to keep on writing.

Thanks to my brothers, Gary and David, for reading the first draft and to Louise for reading a later version.

Thank you to my child readers – Logan and Eloise, who read the book in one of its first draft versions and gave me some feedback.

Many thanks to Erika, who helped me to create my super website.

A special thank you to Debra, who proofread, edited and typeset my book. She guided me patiently through the process and was always willing to edit the book again. I always looked forward to our meetings filled with chat, coffee and cake.

Huge thanks to my daughter, Emily, who was my illustrator and who designed the amazing cover, maps and chapter drawings.

A particular thanks go to my alpha readers, my wonderful mum, Valerie, and my sister, Linda, who painstakingly read and edited my book.

Finally, love and thanks go to my husband, Craig and children, Emily, Christopher and Rebecca (you might notice a wee link with the names!).

Milton Keynes UK
Ingram Content Group UK Ltd.
UKHW040617110624
443927UK00004B/101

9 781738 439201